Health and the En

Health and the Environment

The Linacre Lectures 1992–3

Edited by

BRYAN CARTLEDGE

Principal of Linacre College
University of Oxford

Oxford New York Tokyo

OXFORD UNIVERSITY PRESS

1994 *mah*

Oxford University Press, Walton Street, Oxford OX2 6DP

Oxford   New York
Athens   Auckland   Bangkok   Bombay
Calcutta   Cape Town   Dar es Salaam   Delhi
Florence   Hong Kong   Istanbul   Karachi
Kuala Lumpur   Madras   Madrid   Melbourne
Mexico City   Nairobi   Paris   Singapore
Taipei   Tokyo   Toronto
and associated companies in
Berlin Ibadan

Oxford is a trade mark of Oxford University Press

Published in the United States
by Oxford University Press Inc., New York

A catalogue record for this book is available from the British Library

Library of Congress Cataloging in Publication Data
Health and the environment / edited by Bryan Cartledge. – 1st ed.
(The Linacre lectures: 1992–3)
1. Environmental health.   I. Cartledge, Bryan, Sir. II. Series: Linacre lecture: 1992–3.
RA565.H383 1994   615.9'02–dc20   94–14494
ISBN 0 19 8584180 (Hbk)
ISBN 0 19 8584172 (Pbk)

Typeset by The Electronic Book Factory Ltd, Fife, Scotland

Printed in Great Britain by
Biddles Ltd
Guildford & King's Lynn

NWST

IAGG 9738

Acknowledgements

This third series of Linacre Lectures was the last to be sponsored by the Racal Electronics Group. I should like once again to record the gratitude of Linacre College, and of Oxford University, to Racal for enabling our project to get off the ground in 1990 and then sustaining it for three years. Linacre formed a close working partnership with Racal, both in the context of the lectures and in that of the Racal Studentships which the Group sponsored for the benefit of Russian graduates who wished to undertake research at Oxford in environment-related fields. The partnership worked smoothly in every respect and both sides gained from it.

The Linacre Lectures are continuing under the sponsorship of British Petroleum plc.

I am, once again, immensely grateful to Frances Morphy for her skill and good judgement in preparing our contributors' texts for submission to the Oxford University Press, and not least to Jane Edwards, our College Secretary, for her hard work and crisis management in every aspect of the lecture series to which she devoted, as usual, great energy and enthusiasm.

Linacre College, Oxford   B.G.C.
August 1993

Contents

Authors

Sir Bryan Cartledge, KCMG, MA
Principal, Linacre College, Oxford

Sir Christopher Harding
Chairman, BET plc; formerly Chairman, British Nuclear Fuels Ltd

Dr John Seaman
Head of Overseas Policy Development, The Save the Children Fund

Professor Richard Lacey, MD, PhD, FRCPath
Professor of Medical Microbiology, University of Leeds

Dr John Bowman, CBE
Managing Director, Brown & Root Environmental plc

Professor David Bradley, DM, FRCP, FRCPath, FFCM
Professor of Tropical Hygiene, University of London

Professor Robert May, FRS
Royal Society Research Professor, University of Oxford and Imperial College, London

Professor Sir David Weatherall, FRS
Regius Professor of Medicine, University of Oxford

Sir David Smith, FRS
President, Wolfson College, Oxford

Introduction

Bryan Cartledge

The first two collections of Linacre Lectures—*Monitoring the environment* (OUP 1992) and *Energy and the environment* (OUP 1993)—concentrated on various aspects of the way in which human activity is affecting the long-term future of our planet and its habitability. The focus of this collection is more immediate. Rather than calculating the possibility of significant climatic change in the next century or weighing up the future environmental impact of different sources of energy—both immensely important areas of investigation—most of the lecturers on 'Health and the Environment' were describing problems which are already acute and were becoming more so as they spoke.

An exception is Christopher Harding's contribution on the nuclear power industry, which was designed to link the themes of the previous lecture series, on energy, with those of its successor, on health. His message is that if those countries in a position to do so were to develop nuclear power to its full potential, global CO_2 emissions could be cut by nearly a third, acid rain could be significantly diminished, and gases damaging to the ozone layer could be greatly reduced. This is a rare example of a developmental strategy which could be environmentally benign; rather than pursue it, some Western governments, including our own, have preferred to cast the nuclear industry as the environmental whipping-boy, imposing upon it financial burdens which threaten its viability with the ostensible aim of eliminating a health risk which is infinitesimal compared with those which accumulate from the use of fossil fuels. However, most of the contributors to this volume describe damage to human health which results not from political decisions but from trends in the development of human society which are irresistible and irreversible. Although John Seaman argues convincingly that population growth does not necessarily carry with it the threat of famine, for most others the accelerating rise in world population is the root cause of the threats to health which they describe.

The importance of water—both in quantity and in quality—emerges from several contributions. Growing populations mean a growing demand for food which in turn increases the need for irrigation schemes and dams; these in themselves can be productive of disease and pollution, as David Bradley and John Bowman in particular demonstrate. The urbanization which is the inevitable concomitant of rapid population growth in the developing world brings it own problems, not least, as Robert May shows, in facilitating the spread of infectious diseases and in creating breeding grounds for disease vectors.

Some of the contributions to this volume underline the uncomfortable fact that the adverse impact of a changing environment on the health of a growing population is by no means confined to the developing and newly industrialized countries of the Third World with their teeming cities, vector-breeding lakes and canals, and open sewers. The developed world has new and deeply disturbing problems of its own. Richard Lacey describes the threats to health which have emerged from intensive systems of livestock and poultry breeding, designed to maximize profits from the rapidly expanding market for beef, poultry, and eggs in Western Europe. However vehemently his research may be decried by the farming lobby, the fact remains that, as this Introduction is written (August 1993), confirmed cases of bovine spongiform encephalopathy (BSE) in British herds have exceeded 100 000—a more rapid escalation than even he had forecast. In the light of mounting evidence—including that of a link between BSE and Creutzfeldt–Jakob disease—Professor Lacey's conclusions deserve respect. Moreover, as John Bowman points out, so-called developed countries are capable, through political error or perversity, of generating threats to public health at least as serious as those which are more excusably endemic in the Third World. Dr Bowman rightly cites the case of Eastern Europe; my own direct experience lies further east, in what used to be the Soviet Union, where I spent a large part of my professional life. A few lines about the Communist legacy may not be out of place, not only to underline Dr Bowman's conclusions but also to illustrate many of the points which are made elsewhere in these chapters.

From the outset of Stalin's 'revolution from above', in the early 1930s, the undivided emphasis of the economic strategy of the Soviet regime was on production. All Five Year Plan targets were quantitative; no financial resources were available to factories or farms which could not be justified in terms of increased output. This had many absurd, as well as tragic, consequences: plate-glass factories, for example, were given their Plan targets only in square metres, which meant that they could achieve them, and their bonuses, more easily by producing vast quantities of very thin glass. The windows of Soviet flats were thus prone to crack in extreme temperatures. Quantity was all; quality, either of product (except in the defence industries) or of life for the workforce or of the environment in which they lived, was not merely secondary but irrelevant. Concern for the environment, had any Soviet citizen been rash enough to voice it, would have been dismissed as criminal sentimentality. During Gorbachev's last two years in power, in 1988 and 1989, the glacier of censorship retreated sufficiently to lay bare at least some of the horrifying environmental consequences of the policies of forty years of Stalinist gigantism. Soviet citizens and their representatives were at last free to publicize and discuss the problems which had blighted their cities and regions for decades.

The Aral Sea disaster, because of both its scale and its effect on the populations of most of the Central Asian Soviet Republics, received the lion's share of political and public attention. The two rivers which feed this large inland sea, the Amu Darya and Syr Darya, had been partially diverted in the early 1960s in order to supply water to new irrigation schemes in Uzbekistan and thus boost cotton production. As a result, the Aral Sea began to shrink and by 1988 its level had dropped by 13 metres. The consequential change in the regional microclimate, heavy deposits of wind-blown salt over a vast area to the south and west of the sea, and concomitant deposits of chemical fertilizers, herbicides, and pesticides blown from the drying delta regions on to populated areas had a devastating impact on the health of the local population. A representative of Karakalpakia told the Soviet Congress of People's Deputies on 30 May 1989: 'There has been a sharp rise in the percentage of deformities in new-born babies . . . two out of every three babies examined were ill—mainly with typhoid, cancer of the oesophagus, and hepatitis. There are cases of cholera. In some areas of Karakalpakia doctors do not recommend breast-feeding: the milk is toxic' (BBC Monitoring Report SU/0476, 1989). Two years later, an official report to the Cabinet of Ministers of the newly independent Republic of Kazakhstan confirmed these findings, noting in addition that the genetic stock of flora and fauna was being lost, that living conditions and the health of the population had deteriorated, and that levels of general and infant mortality had risen sharply (*Izvestiya*, 27 November 1991).

Although the Aral Sea joined Lake Baikal (where aquatic life was being gradually exterminated by effluent from a lakeside cellulose plant) as classic examples of the Communist legacy, they were unique only in scale. In Baku the oil refineries and associated plants were found to be discharging 200 kg of pollutants annually for every one of the city's 1 800 000 inhabitants, while in rural Azerbaijan scientists attributed the abnormal incidence of bone disease in newborn babies to the grossly excessive use of pesticides (including DDT) and herbicides in order to maximize grape production. In Nizhny Tagil, an industrial town in the Sverdlovsk region of Russia, the blast furnaces of a metallurgical combine were estimated in 1988 to be depositing 600 tons of pollutants annually on the neighbourhood; high levels of ammonia, formaldehyde, and NO_x in the atmosphere were held responsible for the alarming number of cases of cancer, asthma, bronchitis, and other diseases among the local population. Even in Siberia, the mighty rivers Angara and Yenisei were discovered in 1989 to have been so polluted that most species of fish had been exterminated; in the town of Motygino, on the Angara, 87 per cent of the child population was reported to be suffering from a variety of diseases, most commonly intestinal disorders, eye infections, and hepatitis (Moscow Radio, 28 August 1989). A succession of similar reports from all over the country prompted Dr Yablokov of the Biological Institute of the Academy of Sciences to report to the Congress of People's Deputies on 8 June 1989:

The situation is this: 20 per cent of our country's population live in ecological disaster zones and another 35–40 per cent live in ecologically unfavourable conditions. As a result, the incidence of disease linked to degradation of the quality of the environment is growing rapidly. In our country one in three men suffers from cancer in his lifetime: the number of cancer patients is rising yearly. In a number of regions child mortality is higher than in Africa, while our average life expectancy is four to six years less than in the world's advanced countries (BBC Monitoring Report SU/0485, 1989).

Since then, Russia's death rate has overtaken the birth rate by a significant margin, and infectious diseases thought to have been eradicated, including diptheria and cholera, have reached epidemic levels in some large cities.

This catalogue of disasters, misdeeds, and mismanagement amply confirms Professor Bradley's judgement that 'environment is a massive determinant of disease', but it also shows how an apparently developed country can slip back to Third World status, in terms of public and environmental health, through the pursuit of policies which are misconceived or inhumane or both. Russia is now a democracy, and its elected rulers, like those of other democracies, should heed the wisdom of David Smith's message in the concluding chapter of this volume:

Essentially, there is little prospect that human society will change the way that it behaves to meet important environmental concerns until most people believe that those changes are necessary. Only then will the decisions required achieve political popularity instead of the unpopularity that would greet them today. Achieving this change can only be through education; it cannot be through other forms of 'social engineering'.

Russia and the other former Soviet republics already face a massive process of re-education in most areas of social activity; understanding of and concern for the impact of political, economic, and managerial decisions on the environment, and consequently on the health of the population, should be given a high priority.

The link between health and the environment is not controversial; few readers of this volume will find it novel, although when they have read it they should be better informed as to its nature and diversity. However, there is an important qualification to be made, and David Weatherall makes it. His chapter provides the balance which the Linacre Lectures, series by series, always try to achieve in their treatment of environmental issues—their purpose is by no means simply to provide a soap-box for the Green lobby. Professor Weatherall takes issue with the view that the bulk of the major killers of Western society are due entirely to our unfriendly environment and to our diets and lifestyles. Allowing that where there is solid evidence about the action of particular environmental factors we should do what we can to mitigate them, he argues that we would be unwise to put all our eggs in the environmental basket; rather, we should maintain a two-pronged attack, doing what we can to prevent common diseases by taking corrective environmental action but at the same time encouraging basic research into their causes. Surely, the question of why individual A succumbs to a malady partly or wholly induced by environmental factors while individual B does not is at least as important as the fuller analysis of the links between health and the environment to which most of these Linacre Lectures are devoted.

1

Nuclear power comes clean

Christopher Harding

Sir Christopher Harding is in the forefront of the younger generation of leading British industrialists. An Oxford graduate, he spent eight years with ICI before joining the Hanson Group of companies in 1969. He was appointed Managing Director of the Hanson Transport Group in 1974, at the age of 35. Sir Christopher's association with British Nuclear Fuels (BNFL) began with his appointment to the board of the company in 1984; in 1986 he took over the Chairmanship of BNFL, one of the most politically exposed and controversial positions in British industry. He weathered the vagaries of government policy and the assaults of Green pressure groups with equanimity for eight years, steadily promoting policies of greater openness at Sellafield and in the nuclear industry generally. In 1992 he was appointed Chairman of BET plc.

Sir Christopher Harding's contribution was conceived as a bridge between the second series of Linacre Lectures, 'Energy and the environment' (Oxford University Press, 1993), and this series, on 'Health and the environment'.

I stood down after more than six years as Chairman of BNFL at the end of June 1992, having reached the conclusion that it was time for a change both for me and the company. However, my enthusiasm and commitment to nuclear energy remains unchanged, and what I have to say here is exactly what I would have said had I remained as Chairman of BNFL.

I am very conscious of being something of an odd man out among the distinguished list of contributors to these lectures in that I am not a scientist. Yet I am addressing a subject with a large scientific content. Therefore it will be obvious that I shall be drawing heavily on the work of many other people who *are* scientists and experts in their field, including some of my former colleagues in BNFL.

A word of explanation is due about the title I have chosen. I hope it does not seem too flippant in the context of these lectures. It is intended, as may be suspected, as a play on words covering my two main messages.

- Firstly, nuclear power is a clean and benign form of energy, less threatening to the health and well being of humans and their environment than most other methods of generating electricity.

- Secondly, those who have responsibility for the nuclear industry have belatedly recognized that they must communicate frankly with the public if the technology of nuclear power is to be understood and accepted. 'Coming clean' in this sense means a policy of total candour about the bad news as well as the good. Only by such honesty can the industry hope to earn and retain the trust of the public. 'Cover-up' is about the most damaging accusation that can be levelled at the nuclear industry. It is an accusation that has frequently been made—with some justification on occasion. Nevertheless, I have come to the conclusion that on many past occasions when the charge of covering up was made, and fairly made, the industry's failure to communicate was not due to a wilful desire to deceive, or to pull the wool over people's eyes. I believe that it was more likely to have stemmed from a faint-hearted despair about the industry's ability to make itself understood.

John Rimington, Director-General of the Health and Safety Executive, has made some perceptive comments on this theme in a paper about nuclear safety (Rimington 1988). Theoretical nuclear physics was for many years the queen of the physical sciences. Those who pioneered in this field conveyed an impression of intellectual arrogance, even a claim to moral supremacy, and certainly a feeling that things were going on that were beyond the power of ordinary people to understand. Therefore it was hardly surprising that some of this arrogance communicated itself to those who went on to apply nuclear physics in the military field and then to the generation who undertook the major, and on the whole very beneficial, development of civil nuclear power.

When I joined BNFL, as a layman among a galaxy of highly qualified scientists and engineers, I was very conscious of the gulf in comprehension that had opened up to divide the experts from the general public. I saw it as one of my highest priorities as Chairman to break down the barriers between the two sides. On my first day as BNFL Chairman—1 April 1986, or British Nuclear Fools Day, as Greenpeace chose to dub it—I made the following remarks to the Press:

The fact that a comprehension gulf exists between the nuclear industry and the public, a gulf which so far has not been bridged, does not mean that it is unbridgeable.

A large part of the problem is that those on opposite sides of the gulf do not speak the same language. In our highly technical industry the scientists and the engineers naturally use a technical language of their own. It is short-sighted and indeed arrogant for those in the industry to expect the public to come to terms with their language and jargon.

The traditional response of the nuclear industry to this problem is that somehow we must educate the public to understand what we are saying. I believe the boot is on the other foot. It is we in the industry who have to be educated. Somehow we have to teach ourselves to communicate in language the public can understand. It requires an approach that is not condescending or patronizing but thoughtful and patient.

Since 1986 a great deal of progress has been made not only in BNFL but by the nuclear industry as a whole. In my old company alone more than 500 people, from directors through senior and middle managers to more junior staff who interface directly with the public, have been on presentation courses. The aim of these courses is to help the nuclear community learn how to bridge that comprehension gap by putting things clearly and simply and by telling people what they want to know rather than what we think they ought to know.

We have opened the doors of our plants to the public, particularly at our largest and best known site at Sellafield.

With the help of a new visitors' centre, Sellafield has become one of Britain's major industrial tourist attractions, with an average of over 130 000 visitors a year.

At the centre the latest presentation techniques are used to explain the mysteries of radiation, how nuclear reactors work and are controlled to ensure safe operation, what nuclear fission really means, and how the nuclear industry's wastes are managed to minimize the impact on the environment. Many of Sellafield's visitors, particularly those with special interests, tour the plants themselves, seeing how an industry handling highly hazardous materials protects the health of its workers and the general public by meticulous attention to the construction and operation of its facilities. The guides at our plants have become doubly expert—expert in the technology that they have to explain and expert in the techniques of describing that technology and its effects in understandable form.

'Coming clean' in the communications sense involves more than just learning *how* to communicate, vital though that is. 'Coming clean' is about *what* is communicated as well as how. BNFL faced that issue back in 1986. In my first public statement as Chairman I made, with the full support of my colleagues, a declaration that reflected our conviction that nothing short of total candour could adequately address the legitimate anxieties that had developed about the safety of nuclear power and its implications for health.

The commitment that BNFL gave then was to make information about its activities freely available to anyone who was interested enough to ask—whether they were journalists, politicians, academics, environmentalists, or members of the general public. It is a commitment that BNFL has honoured ever since, and I believe that it has helped significantly to improve its reputation and credibility.

I was delighted to see that my successor as BNFL's Chairman, John Guinness, made it clear at his first Press Conference (24 August 1992) that the policy would continue. BNFL's commitment to its policy of openness and honesty is, he said, irreversible.

Of course we have always made it clear that a few necessary constraints have to be imposed on this free disclosure of information. The industry cannot make public information which would jeopardize national security. BNFL cannot breach necessary commercial or legal confidentiality, and it has to respect the personal privacy of its staff. However, these limitations have been applied sparingly, and I believe that they have been generally understood and accepted.

By way of illustration let me quote a few examples of where we have had to put up the shutters. For instance, in the interests of security BNFL does not give details of how it stores and safeguards stocks of plutonium. Nor, at this moment, is it prepared to disclose detailed information about the current transport arrangements for the return of plutonium to overseas customers—particularly about the long haul by sea to utilities in Japan.

Concern about commercial confidentiality necessitates reticence about some of the details of contracts with customers and negotiations over new ventures. The requirements of legal confidentiality prevent the company from anticipating evidence to be given in pending litigation, such as some cases recently heard in the High Court. These cases are based on claims that Sellafield is responsible for leukaemias among the general public. They have been contested vigorously by BNFL and I shall have more to say on this subject later in this chapter.

Respect for the privacy of employees prevents the company from disclosing details of individuals' medical records without their consent. However, information about the collective health of the workforce is readily available.

I have discussed at some length how the nuclear industry is 'coming clean' in the sense of responding freely to the public's concerns. I now want to turn to some of those concerns, which essentially involve health and safety. The public are right to be concerned about such matters as radiation from the nuclear industry, right in the sense that these are important issues that deserve everyone's attention. However, in my submission, there is no cause for public concern in the sense that equates concern with anxiety. Professionally and meticulously managed, regulated rigorously in the public interest, nuclear power is the most benign and least threatening of all the principal means of electricity generation, with a net positive entry on the environmental balance sheet.

In 1991 nuclear power plants generated 20 per cent of Britain's electricity and did so safely and cleanly. Around the world well over 400 nuclear reactors in 28 countries achieved similar results. Nuclear power accounts for 17 per cent of all the electricity generated in the world, over 22 per cent of that produced in OECD countries, and one-third of the electrical output of the 12 countries of the European Community—even though six of those countries have no nuclear plant.

In May 1992 I attended the World Energy Council's congress in Madrid. That congress, representing leading figures from all the world's energy industries, including those such as coal and gas in direct commercial competition with nuclear power, concluded that 'sustaining and developing the world's capabil-ities to deploy nuclear energy safely and without undue public concern' (World Energy Council 1992) is one of three major activities needed to achieve energy supply with sustainability in mind. The other two are rational energy conservation and the encouragement of renewable energy resources.

What is expected of the nuclear industry if nuclear power is to be developed and deployed safely without undue public concern? There are three key requirements:

(1) to prevent major nuclear accidents;
(2) to minimize radioactive pollution from routine operations and hence limit radiation exposure to the public;
(3) to dispose of nuclear waste without long-term effects on the environment or danger to health. I shall deal with these three issues in turn.

The Chernobyl accident in 1986 was a very serious nuclear accident, about as bad as can be imagined. Thirty-one people died from high radiation doses while fighting the fire. Over 100 000 people living within 30 km of the plant received very significant radiation exposure and the lives of some of them will be shortened by cancer as a result. In addition, a large area of land, around 3000 km², was contaminated and it is not clear when it will be rehabilitated.

The Chernobyl plant was of a type that would not be accepted as safe in the West. Similar plants are now being either modified or withdrawn by the Russians. However, the accident was directly due to perverse maloperation of a kind which Western observers found barely credible. The factors which caused the Chernobyl accident do not apply to nuclear plants in the West. Here we are committed to the strictest attention to safety criteria in design and operation. Such attention can drastically reduce, although it cannot entirely eliminate, the likelihood of a serious nuclear accident.

In Britain the Nuclear Installations Inspectorate pursue safety assessment principles based on twin aims:

- accidents which in practice could conceivably happen have consequences which can be tolerated;
- accidents which could not be tolerated will in practical terms not occur.

Chernobyl was a disaster that few people will forget. How many non-nuclear disasters are remembered in the same way? A former BNFL colleague (Wilkinson 1990) has examined some of the other events of 1986 and discovered that in that year 12 000 people died and two million people were made homeless by more than 200 major accidents. At Bhopal, for example, more than 3 000 people died compared with 30 at Chernobyl and more than 10 000 suffered severe permanent disability.

The crucial safety test that nuclear power has to face, however, is surely this: how do the risks it poses to the health and well-being of the workforce and the public compare with those in other energy industries? A number of comparative risk assessment studies have shown up as a fallacy the popular belief that nuclear power is more hazardous than the alternatives. A recent study (Fritzsche 1989) took account of deaths occurring in all stages of electricity production including fuel extraction and processing, transport, and construction of plant and buildings as well as actual operation. It concluded that risks associated with nuclear power are about two orders of magnitude less than those associated with fossil-fuel plant or renewable energy.

The second requirement that nuclear power must satisfy is minimization of its radioactive pollution and of exposure to radiation. Like any other industry, nuclear power produces waste products as part of its routine operations, some of which are released into the environment. As a result members of the public receive some enhancement to the radiation dose to which they are exposed. Figure 1.1, which is a chart produced by the National Radiological Protection Board (NRPB), demonstrates that radioactivity was not invented by the nuclear industry. There is a lot of it about, most of it of entirely natural origin.

Eighty-seven per cent of our radiation exposure in the United Kingdom is due to naturally occurring radioactivity. Of the

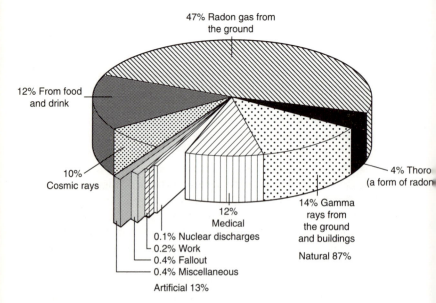

Fig. 1.1. The origin of radioactivity in the environment.

remaining 13 per cent, medical radiotherapy and diagnosis accounts for all but 1 per cent. The radiation exposure resulting directly from the nuclear industry amounts to less than 0.1 per cent—one-thousandth of the total.

These figures are based on the average exposure to the British population. Some people are exposed to larger doses, and since most of the exposure resulting from nuclear operations comes from the reprocessing of spent nuclear fuel at Sellafield, the members of the public most heavily exposed from this source are a very small number living close to Sellafield itself.

The maximum radiation exposure permitted from the nuclear industry is based on the advice of the International Commission on Radiological Protection, an independent expert body. In Britain the NRPB, based at Chilton in Oxfordshire, interprets this guidance and advises the Government what limitations it should place on the nuclear industry's discharges of radioactivity in order to ensure that the permitted maximum exposures to people are not exceeded.

For many years it was enough for the managers of nuclear plants to ensure that they kept within the numerical maxima placed by Government authorization on their discharges. That is not enough today. The principal protective measure to limit public exposure has now become the additional requirement to keep discharges as low as reasonably achievable using best practical means. That means applying the best available technology not entailing excessive cost—BATNEEC in the unlovable language of the regulators.

The limitations to radiation exposure which these regulations are designed to achieve apply to the most affected members of the public. The task of identifying this group falls to the Ministry of Agriculture, Fisheries and Food (MAFF) who conduct habit surveys to establish exposure both directly and by ingestion through the very diverse food chains that apply to agriculture and fishery produce.

For low level liquid discharges of radioactivity to the sea from Sellafield the critical group consists of a small number of individuals who consume locally gathered and locally caught seafoods in substantial quantity. The consumption habits of this critical group are, to put it mildly, extreme. For example, their annual diet includes 8 kg of the flesh of locally caught winkles. To determine the extent to which the foods eaten by the critical group are contaminated by radioactivity, extensive programmes of monitoring and analysis are conducted by BNFL and, as an independent check, by scientists employed by MAFF. The results of both surveys are very consistent. BNFL publishes each year full details of its discharges, its monitoring, and the resultant exposures to the public. A popular version of this report receives very wide circulation.[1] In fact the critical group receives from Sellafield less than half the current advisory limit for exposure, and less than a tenth of the exposure which, on average, we all receive from natural radiation.

Radioactivity differs from other pollutants in two important respects: it can be readily measured, down to the most minute amounts, and the relationship between radiation and health effects is well established.

Dr Steve Jones of BNFL has described the health effects of radiation exposure in a paper to the World Energy Council. (Jones 1992). Generally, they can be divided into two types. For very large acute doses of radiation, sufficient biological damage is caused to produce obvious early clinical symptoms (radiation burns) or even death due to the disruption of essential biological processes. This is what happened to the firemen at Chernobyl. These effects are termed 'deterministic' and are characterized by the existence of a very large threshold radiation dose below which the effects do not occur. At lower doses radiation can cause more subtle changes in cell function which can ultimately give rise to cancers or genetic defects. These effects are termed 'stochastic' and are characterized by the probability of the effect being proportional to the dose received. It is assumed that there is no threshold for these effects and that each small increment in dose represents an increment in the risk. The assumption of a

---

[1] Health, Safety and the Environment, Annual Report, British Nuclear Fuels Ltd.

linear relationship between risk and dose, with no threshold, is a cautious position which may overstate the risk associated with low doses. Nevertheless, it is the basis on which decisions about the regulation of risks from radioactivity, and on the control of nuclear industry operations, are taken.

Similar assumptions could be made, but generally are not, in relation to the regulation of low level exposure to other pollutants. Using the considerable data on human exposure to radiation and this 'linear hypothesis', limits are set which are designed to keep the risk of late stochastic effects of exposure to a low and acceptable level. If these limits are observed it will be impossible to observe any stochastic effects in the exposed population because the frequency of radiation-induced effects will be orders of magnitude lower than the natural frequency with which such effects occur. This practice is much more cautious than that adopted for control of many other hazardous materials, where the extensive data and research necessary to quantify stochastic effects of exposure are often simply not available. Therefore the public is better protected from the risks of nuclear power than from other potentially hazardous industries.

Discharges of low level radioactivity to the sea at Sellafield have been reduced to just 1 per cent of the levels at which they were running in the 1970s. This reduction has been achieved by the introduction of a new pollution control plant at Sellafield costing some £700 million.

In my view we have reached—indeed we have already passed—the point at which the requirements on the nuclear industry to reduce its pollution further have moved so far out of line with those placed on other industries as to defy reason. Each further step in reducing discharges costs progressively more to achieve, and this law of diminishing returns means that the benefit from the last £200 million BNFL is spending on discharge reduction will be to save just two theoretical lives in the next 10 000 years.

It is not really a case of special pleading by the nuclear industry to say that there are more sensible ways of spending money. There are far more effective ways in which to spend money in order to reduce the public's exposure to radiation. The cost to BNFL of reducing the population exposure by 1 man-Sievert (the unit of collective radiation dose) is about £1 million. The same reduction could be achieved by replacing inefficient X-ray equipment in hospitals at a cost of £9000 (Haywood 1988). As an independent expert adviser has said: 'If there existed any logic, then resources would be put into reducing medical exposures rather than in reducing the already low discharges from Sellafield' (Boddy 1989).

Now, to justify the claim of a clean bill of health for the nuclear industry it is necessary to consider the health of those who work in the industry as well as that of the general public. Workers are permitted to receive, and do receive, larger exposures from nuclear operations than do the general public. However, we should note that many members of the public receive far larger *total* doses of radiation than any nuclear worker is permitted to receive. This is simply because they live in parts of the country, like Cornwall, with high levels of natural radiation, mainly from the build-up of radon gas in their homes.

The latest findings by the NRPB (Kendall *et al.* 1992) demonstrate that nuclear workers are a healthy group. Their life expectancy is greater than that of the general British public. The well-known 'healthy worker' effect is clearly a factor here, as it is with most occupations, since the general public obviously includes a proportion of those who are too ill or too disabled to work, which an occupational group does not. However, given the accepted link between radiation exposure and cancer causation, the really significant feature of health studies of nuclear workers is that they show that the nuclear workforce has a significantly reduced risk of dying of cancer. The one exception to this is a small additional risk that they bear of dying from leukaemia, itself a rare cause of death.

This study by the NRPB is based on records of dose and causes of death from the National Registry of Radiation Workers. It covers an industry whose history goes back more than 40 years. It includes occupational dose levels that would not be tolerated today. As Roger Berry, BNFL's former director of health and safety, put it when the report was published: 'It provides evidence that current radiation protection practice is at least good enough' (Berry 1992).

The NRPB study was notable in identifying a correlation among nuclear workers between lifetime exposure and the risk of developing leukaemia—the first time such a phenomenon has been observed. It is, of course, consistent with the assumption underlying the principles of radiological protection—risk is proportional to exposure.

Many nuclear workers, past and present, die of cancer. In most cases it can be assumed that their occupation had no bearing on their death. After all, cancer accounts for more than one in four of all deaths in the general population. In a minority of cases, however, the possibility arises that radiation exposure at work, perhaps as a result of a particular incident involving unusually high exposure, may have been a factor.

Claims of this kind are difficult to substantiate in a court of law where standards of proof require demonstration of a probability of cause and effect greater than 50 per cent. For that reason, acting as good employers, BNFL in association with the trade unions operates a voluntary compensation scheme which provides a sliding scale of compensation proportional to the probability that radiation is a causal factor. Decisions are based on the views of an independent panel of doctors.

The issues of radiation exposure to the general public and occupational exposure to the nuclear workforce are drawn together in considering current allegations that leukaemias among children and young people in West Cumbria are associated with radiation from Sellafield. At the heart of the allegations is an excess of childhood leukaemias identified over a period of time in the village of Seascale, the nearest community to Sellafield. The number of individual cases was small, but in so small a community it represented an incidence of the disease ten times what might have been expected. The leukaemias are a fact. The cause of them remains a mystery. According to most experts radioactive discharges from Sellafield can be ruled out.

On the most cautious assumptions discharges would have had to be greater by two orders of magnitude to be held responsible.

A new hypothesis was put forward in a report published by the late Professor Martin Gardner of Southampton University (Gardner *et al.* 1990). In a statistical epidemiological study he identified a link between some childhood leukaemias and occupational exposure received before conception by the fathers, who were workers at Sellafield. No such link has ever been shown up by other studies, and the Gardner hypothesis has been greeted with scepticism by most geneticists. Sir Richard Doll, perhaps the world's leading epidemiologist, believes that the Gardner findings are most probably due to chance (Doll 1992).

Nor is the Gardner hypothesis supported by other studies, the most recent of which is a survey undertaken in Canada (McLaughlin 1992). A team looked at 112 cases of childhood leukaemia in proximity to five nuclear plants in Ontario, where incidentally no excess leukaemia incidence was present. They found no association between the leukaemias and the radiation exposure of fathers, and added (McLaughlin *et al.* 1992):

The findings of this study are not consistent with the hypothesis that childhood leukaemia is associated with the occupational exposure of fathers to radiation prior to conception, as was found by Gardner.

The issue of whether there is or is not any link between the nuclear power industry and the incidence of leukaemia in the general public remains unresolved, as does the question of what other factor, apart from radiation, might be the cause if such a link is confirmed. Chemical toxicity, virus infection, and social class differentiation are among possible causal factors that have been suggested.

It should be remembered that the number of cases in question is small, which limits the power of the epidemiologists to throw light on the issue. At least one medical scientist, an experimental haematologist, questions for this very reason how much further epidemiological studies—dealing with the incidence, distribution, and control of disease in a population—can take the current line of research (Wright 1992):

Rather than giving precise correlations and neat answers, epidemiology's role has been to alert us to some of the possibilities. What we have to do now is get into experimental approaches, asking what actually happens when you expose appropriate cells to very low doses of radiation.

It is clear that, despite the considerable research being devoted to this problem, it will be a long time before medical science produces firm answers to all the questions about leukaemia causation. Meanwhile, the law has been asked to come up with answers of its own in two cases which occupied the High Court for the best part of a year. The plaintiffs' lawyers relied heavily on the Gardner hypothesis but the judge concluded, on the balance of probabilities, that pre-conception radiation was not the cause of the Seascale leukaemias. Judgement was given, therefore, in BNFL's favour.

The allegations about Sellafield which lay behind the litigation received massive publicity, much of it highly emotional, in the Press and on television. Every leukaemia case is a human tragedy which causes great distress to the families of the victims. This distress was renewed for these families by the gruelling processes of the law.

Why did not BNFL save those concerned this distress by settling these cases out of court? To settle, it was argued, would cost the company far less than the £10 million which is the estimated total costs it will have to meet arising from the litigation. BNFL's reply is clear. While it has every sympathy for the families concerned, who have close links with the company, it says that it has the overwhelming weight of expert opinion on its side and that the issue is too important for the whole nuclear industry to be allowed to go by default.

I now turn to the third of the three major requirements that the nuclear industry must satisfy if it is to be given that clean bill of health which is of vital importance to its future development. This is to demonstrate its ability to provide safe disposal of its radioactive waste.

Nuclear waste is commonly regarded by the public and many politicians as an unsolved problem which, if it is not solved, threatens the future of the nuclear industry. Such a view is entirely wrong. The only major unsolved problems concerning radioactive waste are ones of perception and location—of identifying and confirming the suitability of specific sites to meet the technical requirements for safe disposal, and securing public and political acceptance for specific disposal projects in specific places. For the rest, the technology is readily available to engineer underground disposal facilities, and at Sellafield plants to put all the waste in suitable form for disposal have been built and are working.

The volumes of radioactive waste are small compared with all the other domestic and industrial waste produced by a modern industrialized society. According to figures assembled by the British Nuclear Forum (1992), each year Britain produces over four million cubic metres of toxic waste alone—enough to fill seven skyscrapers on the scale of Canary Wharf. Only one-hundredth of that is radioactive waste. High level waste, which accounts for 95 per cent of the radioactivity amounts only to 40 cubic metres, i.e. enough to fill a small lorry.

In volume terms most of the nuclear industry's waste is low level—paper towels, disposable clothing, laboratory trash, and the like. For over 30 years waste of this kind has been disposed of at BNFL's Drigg site near Sellafield. The waste is now packed in containers, which are then placed in concrete vaults. Eventually these containers will be grouted into a solid block and topped with a concrete cover. With full compaction of the waste, the life of Drigg will now extend towards the middle of the next century.

Just over a tenth of all radioactive waste in volume terms is of intermediate level—swarf cladding from nuclear fuel elements and other material. It is a thousand times more radioactive than low level waste. The new Magnox Encapsulation Plant, built at Sellafield at a cost of £250 million, mixes the swarf in concrete and seals it in stainless steel drums. The drums are stored in a surface store to await eventual disposal. At least two more surface stores will need to be built at Sellafield to cope with intermediate waste before the year 2007, when it is hoped that a deep repository will be available to receive the drums for underground emplacement.

At the top end of the radioactive waste spectrum comes high level waste—the fission products from reprocessing, stored as a liquid. This waste represents only about one-thousandth of the total volume, but accounts for 95 per cent of the radioactivity. It is a thousand times more active than intermediate waste. A new vitrification plant is now glassifying this waste at Sellafield, reducing the volume to a third in the process. This highly sophisticated plant, which cost some £250 million, casts the molten radioactive glass in stainless steel containers like giant milk churns and sends them to the vitrified product store where they are stacked in self-cooling channels. The high level waste associated with the United Kingdom nuclear programme will remain there for at least 50 years. By the end of that period, because of the decay of short-lived radionuclides, heat generation and radiation will be much reduced and this will simplify subsequent disposal. Waste from overseas customers' fuel will be shipped back to the countries of origin.

About £2000 million has been spent on radioactive waste management plants at Sellafield in recent years. This is a technology in which the British nuclear industry leads the world. Thus the radioactive waste scene is vastly different from the popular conception of mountains of menacing material growing in an uncontrollable way, with the nuclear industry at a loss over how to tackle the problem.

Most of the milestones along the road to a complete solution are already in place. The last step will be to obtain planning consent for Britain's first underground nuclear waste repository, which is intended to be sited alongside the reprocessing plant at Sellafield. Permission to start work on this project will depend on establishing by further drilling and underground survey that the host rock is sufficiently stable for the purpose.

The project itself is a major one. Total costs of construction and operation are estimated at £2500 million, with a construction workforce peaking at 3000. It will meet Britain's needs as a national depository for intermediate waste for the next half century, and will hold its radioactivity secure against harmful return to the human environment for the many thousands of years necessary for the activity to decay away.

This long-term entrapment or containment of the radioactivity contained in the waste, and the associated regulatory target, will be achieved by using a multiple-barrier approach. The barriers to minimize migration of radionuclides from the emplaced waste are provided by the engineered components of the repository and by the specific choice of geological siting.

The man-made features will consist of the waste immobilization media in which the waste components are embedded (typically concrete as in the containers filled at Sellafield with intermediate waste), the waste packages themselves (stainless steel drums), the vault structure of the repository, and the backfill in which the containers will be grouted when emplacement is complete. These man-made features will provide a very high level of containment for several hundred years. After that what are called 'far-field' barriers are provided naturally by the geological surroundings. Choosing a location with very slow rates of water movement, for instance, will inhibit migration of radioactivity by groundwater pathways.

Before permission can be given to develop the radioactive waste repository proposed at Sellafield, or anywhere else for that matter, a public inquiry will investigate every technical aspect of the proposal as well as giving a hearing to objectors, whether they are environmental activists or simply local people who do not welcome as a neighbour what the Press tends to call a 'nuclear dump'.

The derogatory word 'dump' hardly fits the high standards of engineering or the exacting regulatory requirements associated with a radioactive waste repository. Assessment of the radiological impact is a vital part of the planning procedure, even though the radiological significance of repository operations will be small compared with a nuclear power station or a nuclear chemical plant.

Guidelines laid down by the regulatory authorities require that radioactive exposure to any member of the public over time-scales of at least 10 000 years should be no more than 0.1 millisieverts (mSv) per year—about a twenty-fifth of the typical total radiation dose of anyone living in Britain. Put another way, it is about a twentieth of the extra dose an airline stewardess would receive per year from the increased cosmic radiation at high altitudes.

However, interest in the radiological effects of a waste repository extends much further in time than a few thousand years. Predictive modelling has been applied on a time-scale of up to 10^8 (100 million) years following closure of a repository. On this basis it has been estimated that the highest possible dose to the public would be 0.06 mSv per year—equivalent to three chest X-rays. I should add that this maximum effect would occur under fairly adverse environmental and social conditions—an ice age in which the local population would be pursuing a subsistence existence as hunter–gatherers. In such circumstances mankind would have greater and more immediate problems than the radiological effects of a Sellafield waste repository.

In this chapter I have dealt with what are commonly regarded as the adverse effects of nuclear power—safety risks, radioactive pollution, and consequential radiation exposure—and with the question of radioactive waste. My aim has been to show that the benefits of nuclear fission as a source of electricity, virtually limitless in terms of earth resources, need not pose unacceptable risks to human health and well-being, and indeed do not present risks greater than those accepted from other industrial activities.

However, all that is to claim no more than a neutral effect for nuclear power on the environmental balance sheet. I want to go further than that. Nuclear power has positive environmental advantages to its credit which justify the claim that the uranium atom is the cleanest and most benign of all the major sources of electricity available to us. The claim is based on the fact that nuclear power makes no contribution to some of the most damaging forms of pollution that the world faces, all of which are associated with burning fossil fuels.

- Nuclear power does not create acid rain which kills off forests and their wildlife and makes lakes and rivers sterile.
- Nuclear power does not emit the gases which punch holes in the ozone layer at the poles—holes which seem to be growing and are now extending to areas of human habitation.
- Above all, nuclear power does not produce CO_2 which is widely believed to be threatening the world environment from an enhanced greenhouse effect.

Scientific opinion is divided on whether the last of these is a real or imaginary threat. Unfortunately, only time will provide the definitive answer to that question. If the pessimistic view should turn out to be correct, it will by then probably be too late to prevent major and probably irreversible effects on the world climate. These effects, produced by apparently quite small increases in average temperatures, could well be disastrous to whole populations, causing inundation, desertification, and famine. As an editorial in the New Scientist (15 May 1986) has put it: 'Implications for agriculture as rainfall and temperature patterns change, and for coastal regions as sea levels rise, are likely to be as profound over the next century, as all the hazards of nuclear power put together'.

Faced with this awful uncertainty prudent governments around the world have decided that it would be wise to play safe and start restricting CO_2 emissions. This can only be achieved by enormous changes in the way that energy is used i.e. curbing demand by greater energy efficiency, and in the way that energy is produced. The Toronto Conference on the Changing Climate (1992) called on governments to cut greenhouse gas emissions by 50 per cent with an initial global aim of reducing CO_2 emissions by 20 per cent of current levels by 2005.

At a time when the world's most populous nations, including China and India, are planning huge increases in fossil-fuel consumption this is probably wishful thinking—'pie in the sky' seems a reasonably apt metaphor. However, there are ways in which the industrialized nations could make a significant contribution towards those targets—by meeting rising demand for electricity with nuclear power and by a process of substituting nuclear power for existing fossil-fuel generation plant as the opportunity arises.

The relative emissions of CO_2 from different sources of electricity generation (Fig. 1.2) show what could be achieved by this process. If nuclear power continues to grow at its present slow rate, it might be generating about a fifth of the world's electricity by the third decade of the 21st century. At this level it would be saving about four billion tonnes of CO_2—12 per cent of what would otherwise be emitted—but, sadly, the world's total CO_2 emissions would still be significantly greater, not less, than those of today. However, if the world's nuclear programme was expanded to the limits, nuclear stations *could* be producing half the world's electricity by then, reducing CO_2 emissions by 30 per cent of what they otherwise would have been.

The nuclear industry has never claimed that it alone can solve the problems of the greenhouse effect. However, it has the power—it *is* the power—to *help* to solve them. In my view

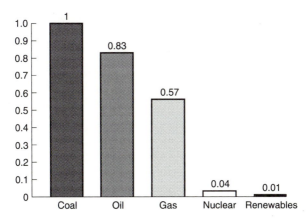

Fig. 1.2. Relative CO_2 emissions per unit of electricity.

it would be an act of omission and of grave irresponsibility not to use that power to its full potential, knowing, as I have sought to show, that it is an energy source with which we can live without fear.

REFERENCES

Berry, R. (1992). *New Scientist*, **14 March**.

Boddy, K. (1989). Report by independent adviser to the Sellafield Local Liaison Committee.

British Nuclear Forum (1992). *Nuclear Forum*, **February** (3).

Doll, R. (1992). British Nuclear Energy Conference on Radiation Effects, May 1992.

Fritzsche, A. F. (1989). The health risks of energy production. *Risk Analysis*, 565–77

Gardner, M. J., *et al.* (1990). Results of case–control study of leukaemia and lymphoma among young people near Sellafield. *British Medical Journal*, **300**, **February**, 423–9.

Haywood, J. K. (1988). *Bulletin of the Hospital Physics Association*, **June** (17–19).

Jones, S. R. (1992). The environmental impact of nuclear power. *15th Congress of the World Energy Council, Madrid, September 1992*.

Kendall, G. M., *et al.* (1992) NRPB Report R251.

McLaughlin, J. R., *et al.* (1992). *Occupational exposure of fathers to ionising radiation and the risk of leukaemia in offspring*. Atomic Energy Control Board, Ottawa.

Rimington, J. (1988). *Civil nuclear power: how safe is safe enough?* Clean Air Society, London.

Wilkinson, W. L. (1990). Paper presented at Conference on Pollution Management, Birmingham, October 1990.

World Energy Council (1992). *15th Congress of the World Energy Council, Madrid, September 1992*.

Wright, E. (1992). *Nucleonics Week*, **24 September**.

2

Population, food supply, and famine: an ecological or an economic dilemma?

John Seaman

Dr John Seaman is Head of Overseas Policy Development for the Save the Children Fund. After training and qualifying in paediatric medicine at the London Hospital, he spent twenty years working overseas in the fields of emergency relief and economic development. His first experience of food crisis was in Biafra during the Nigerian civil war; food crisis subsequently became his dominant interest and speciality. Dr Seaman joined Save the Children in 1979. He has contributed numerous articles on the management of emergencies to academic and medical journals, including the journal 'Disasters' (Blackwell, Oxford).

INTRODUCTION

By the year 2060, world population is expected approximately to double from the current figure of around 5.5 billion to about 11 billion people. On the highest estimate, population may nearly triple, and only under the most favourable and unlikely conditions can we expect population to stabilize at approximately 8 billion people (UN Population Fund 1992). In a world which is already crowded, in which species are being extinguished daily, and where pollution and environmental degradation are already at alarming levels, it seems inconceivable that this growth in population can occur without a major calamity.

There are, of course, many views as to the form that this calamity might take. These range from the extinction of the elephant and other species, from the felling of forests and the pressure of human settlement on land, through large-scale flooding and the complete disappearance of some countries as greenhouse warming expands the oceans, to the extreme possibility of the total extinction of life on the planet. The last possibility, which might occur if global warming leads to the melting of the northern permafrost, does not seem to be entirely hypothetical. Moreover, the explosion of population has raised an old spectre: that population, if it has not done so already in some parts of the world, must soon outrun its food supply—the Malthusian famine may be at hand.

There is a wide range of published opinion on the relationship between population, environment, and food supply. Very roughly classified by source, these opinions fall into three groups: political views, the views of academics, and the perspective of development specialists and agencies.

Politicians, or at least those in recent British Governments, seem convinced of future famine. For example, the last Prime Minister, Lady Thatcher, has argued in favour of British membership of the European Community (EC) to avoid being left 'at the end of the "global food queue"'. John Selwyn Gummer, then Minister of Agriculture, speaking on the BBC on 27 September 1992 on the subject of set-aside land and defending the continuation of European intervention stocks, did this on the basis that 'he did not wish to be remembered, in ten to fifteen years time, when global food supplies were getting short, as the Minister of Agriculture who had left the UK short of food'.

In contrast, political views from the developing countries, although increasingly registering concern about population, tend to downplay the importance of this in favour of the relative importance of economic development. This argument, strongly advanced at the 1992 Rio de Janeiro Global Summit on the environment, was that environmental degradation was the product of poverty, and that the environment could be best maintained by a population wealthy enough to do so, as in the industrialized countries, not by simply reducing the absolute number of people living in want.

Academic views, as might be expected, generally reflect the narrower perspective of a particular discipline. At the risk of overgeneralization and with the additional proviso that most academic views emanate from the industrialized countries, it is probably fair to say that these are, subject by subject, no less gloomy. The conclusion is that too many people means too little food, whether this is taken from the perspective of rates of change in production by the erosion of land, or the probable reduction of productivity in a greenhouse world. One calculation of the effects of a greenhouse world on food supply crudely set against gross world population is that the number of hunger-related deaths might, on some assumptions, be expected to double to 400 million each year (Daily and Erlich 1990.). It may be relevant to note here that similar prognostications made in the early 1970s, and which should now be a current reality, have proved to be false (Erlich 1971).

However, there are exceptions. One such is Sir Alan Walters, previously economic adviser to the British Government, who has on record his view that population growth is a positive economic advantage. In the *London Evening Standard* (8 June 1992) he wrote:

In the 1970s and 1980s, the production of food grains far outstripped population growth. Of course, there were heart-rending famines in Ethiopia and the Sudan, etc., but these were the result of Marxist expropriation . . . Even today's famine in Southern Africa, although caused largely by an unusually severe drought, has been much exacerbated by countries such as Zimbabwe fixing below-market prices for its State monopoly trading agency's acquisition of millet.

Leaving on one side the fact that the Sudan has never had a Marxist government and that the principal cereal crop of Zimbabwe is maize, the argument is easy to support. Figures from the UN Food and Agriculture Organization show that, since 1970, there has been a progressive rise in food energy availability per person and a fall in the proportion of 'chronically underfed people' in all regions of the world except Africa, where the figure has remained roughly constant.

Lastly, for completeness, there are the views of development specialists and agencies. These are rather harder to classify but include those with a more or less declared position—an agency named Population Concern, or perhaps for that matter the Save the Children Fund might be considered to have made its position relatively clear—but we can make a reasonable, if broad, division between government development agencies, which tend to emphasize the population view and the desirability of family planning, and the more developmental non-government agencies in the industrialized and developing countries which, although generally accepting the need for family planning, tend to take the economic view that if people were better off the problem would not be there.

Of course, all these views, except perhaps the academic, can easily be dismissed as simply partisan. Politicians from industrialized and poor countries, or for that matter development agencies, might be expected to take a predictable stance based on their vested interests. However, we are still left with the question: what is the most productive position to take with respect to population, food supply, and the environment, now and into a foreseeable future? Which of the two perspectives—population control or economy—is more helpful if we wish to prevent the apparent inevitability of starvation on an increasing scale and frequency? We can clearly begin by agreeing that the two options are not mutually exclusive. Population clearly is a problem—it is hard to look at South-east England without coming to that conclusion—and countries such as China have combined formidable economic growth with draconian measures to limit population growth. However, from an international perspective and keeping the poorer developing countries in mind, which perspective is likely to be the most productive—'population control', through the distribution of contraceptives, or 'development'?

THE MALTHUSIAN POPULATION MODEL

As a framework for discussion, I shall use the original model of population dynamics derived by Malthus and first published in 1798. The name of Malthus is perhaps best known in terms of the 'Malthusian famine'—a famine which occurs because of an excess of population over food supply. Malthus calculated that if population increases in a geometric fashion—he calculated it as being capable of doubling every twenty-five years or so—and food supply increases roughly linearly, population must increase beyond the means of subsistence. To summarize Malthus's views is difficult—he wrote a great deal and, like many academics, developed his ideas over time—but from the perspective of our subject it is probably fair to say that his interest was not so much in why population should exceed its food supply, but why in fact it does not always, or even very often, seem to do so. To quote Malthus (Penguin edition, 1982):

It follows . . . that the average rate of actual increase of population . . . obeying the same laws as the increase of food must be of a totally different character to the rate at which it would increase *if unchecked*. The great question then . . . is the manner in which this . . . check . . . practically operates.

In short, population may increase beyond its food supply and be cut back, or it may not increase to that point at all. Malthus postulated two types of check on population growth. The first—the 'positive checks'—included war, pestilence, and famine. The second—the two 'preventive checks'—were moral restraint, which in the world of his time was essentially delayed marriage, and the 'unwholesome manufactures' or contraceptives, of which he clearly disapproved.

Malthus was wrong in some respects about the application of his model. For example, he might be surprised that since his time the population of Great Britain has grown from approximately 10 million to the current 50 million and has yet to outrun its food supply (and not, it should be noted, because it simply imports more food). The United Kingdom still produces substantially more food energy than it consumes. We trade for food to avoid a diet which would otherwise be mostly cereals and mutton. However, we can concede that Malthus was right to the extent that there may be some limit set by food production on the growth of population. If 50 million British is not enough, perhaps 100 million will be; Malthus may simply have supposed that the limit was rather stricter than it turned out to be. The basic model is still useful.

To return to our dilemma, the Malthusian model leads to three questions. Firstly, why do famines occur? Specifically, is this because of a shortage of food? Incidentally, we may also ask if modern famines are a significant check on population. Secondly, what is the relationship between food supply and population? Do more and more people, as common sense would tell us, mean less food, more destruction of the environment, and inevitable mass starvation? Lastly where, if anywhere, does food supply fit into Malthus's preventive checks: why do people have more or less children and does the availability of food fit into this argument at all?

FAMINE IN THE MODERN WORLD

It is often argued in the media that famine-prone areas of the world are over-populated, and that this is the cause of modern famines. However, if we accept this view there are two characteristics of famine which may seem paradoxical to anyone who has seen reports of recent African famine in the media.

Famine is a very rare phenomenon even in the 'famine continent' of Africa. Over the last two decades, it is possible to find perhaps ten cases, certainly no more than a dozen, which could reasonably be described in these terms. Several of these ten cases were relatively local and small scale—for example, the death of a few hundred people in parts of the northern Sahel during drought. Cases of mass starvation, for instance in Ethiopia in the mid-1980s where famine caused hundreds of thousands of deaths, have been very rare in modern times. Also, within any famine area, the proportion of people who die tends to be rather small, typically no more than a few per cent of the population.

On current evidence, we have to conclude that in twenty years in a vast, populous, and mostly impoverished continent, suffering the worst climatic change in recorded history, the risk to any individual of dying in a famine has been very small. For example, the 1973 famine in Ethiopia, which was the international *cause célèbre* of its day, killed directly and indirectly (many famine deaths are from disease rather than directly from starvation) about 4 per cent of the population within the area affected by drought, over and above the number who might have been expected to die in the period concerned. This is not to trivialize the case; in this case 4 per cent is approximately 40 000 people, and a larger proportion were displaced or economically destroyed. However, it raises a question about what is going on: how do we reconcile the rarity of famine, even in very poor countries, and the relatively low mortality which results even where there has been a catastrophic and often protracted failure of production?

The reasons for this are now well understood and can be summarized by stating that the problem of famine is not simply one of the quantity of food in an area or country relative to the population. Rather, it is a result of the way in which people gain or fail to gain access to the food which is available. The extreme rarity of large-scale starvation is due to the fact that, even if people in industrialized countries do not understand this, people in poor countries do, and they arrange their affairs accordingly.

Poor people in risky environments engage in a variety of economic strategies. Essentially, this involves the diversification of income from agriculture, labour, and trade, the storage of food, to minimize the risk of exposure to rising prices, to a very variable extent the redistribution of food within society by gifts and loans of food and productive assets and, when times are hard, movement out of the area to find work, charity, or relief. To starve an African, particularly in those areas where the risk of drought and other hazards is highest and people are best prepared, requires a special combination of circumstances, which almost by definition only rarely arises. Typically, it requires a protracted failure of production (for example, from several years of drought), a sufficient proportion of people unable to convert their capital and savings into food because of the collapse of prices, and often the accident of war or special difficulties of geography.

It is no surprise that the rare famines of modern times have occurred in the few remaining economically isolated areas such as highland Ethiopia, or where people have been isolated physically, or their stocks destroyed, or trade obstructed by war. A relevant observation is that many of the people who were made destitute or died in the 1973 Ethiopian famine and in some other locations were not the poorest. They were poor by our measures but by the measure of their own country were secure—for example, they owned land, some livestock, and possibly a gun. In an area of recent settlement they had simply not organized their economy to meet that contingency and lacked the skills to survive when crisis came. For the poorest, such skills are rehearsed every year.

To generalize, it is clear that the same situation would hold even if the amount of food in a famine area was less than that required by the whole population. For example, a case can be made that in the 1984–5 Ethiopian famine, which affected a similar but larger area than that in 1973, all the food in at least the most severely affected area, divided by the population, would have resulted in too little food for each person to allow more than short-term survival. However, the problem remains the same: there was plenty of food in surrounding areas and overseas—some of which was later brought in as relief—and there was a vast and largely successful migration of people out of the area to find work and food. Even in this case, much complicated by war, we need to ask why a proportion of the people were unable to obtain food, not why there was no food to be found.

The true nature of the problem can be seen in its most extreme form in the rare cases of death by starvation in the UK—most commonly those occur in derelicts diagnosed as suffering from exposure. There is obviously no contradiction between this and a European food mountain measured in millions of tons.

As a check on world population, the effect of famine is so small as to be insignificant. The effect may be larger, within an area affected by famine but even here the check on population is rapidly made good by natural population increase. In a severe case, such as the 1985 Ethiopian famine, the loss of population within the area might be made up in perhaps four or five years. Indeed, the remarkable feature of such an area is its biological success, with population steadily increasing in the face of worsening poverty, migration, and catastrophe.

To return to the point made by Sir Alan Walters, that increasing population is a positive good in terms of food supply, it is the case that in some parts of Africa famine has become rarer as a result of increasing population density, even where climate and soils have deteriorated. For example, there is good reason to believe that famine in Darfur in Western Sudan in the early part of this century was more severe than in the 1980s and that it has virtually disappeared from Southern Asia. Even in areas where agricultural production has fallen through drought, greater population has allowed the development of a larger economy, roads, transport, trade, and all the machinery of redistribution.

In a world economy in which some people do not produce the food they consume, the idea of food shortage has so far become a reality only in areas where an economy is wholly isolated from its surroundings, or where because of a lack of effective demand or inadequate systems of redistribution some people cannot obtain food. In the modern world, the first set of conditions is for all practical purposes confined to remote bands of forest Indians, cities under siege, and populations otherwise isolated by war; the second is a matter of poverty and the instability of free markets. However, conditions of global shortage potentially exist, and it is to this question, the adequacy of current and probable future global food supplies, that I now turn.

CURRENT AND PROJECTED WORLD FOOD SUPPLIES

How much food is there in the world relative to need? Is there any real reason to suppose that we are reaching the limit of production?

The answer to the first of these questions is clear. Global food production, taking food-grains alone, is approximately two billion tons per annum. Assuming that four people can reasonably subsist on a ton for a year—an allocation rather more generous than is available to many people in the developing countries— the current food supply would be enough to feed around 8 billion people, i.e. 30 per cent or so more than the current total. Currently, the surplus is largely consumed by livestock for the production of a constant supply of meat, independent of the season, or is converted to alcohol, or finds a variety of other industrial uses. The available surplus, largely in the industrialized countries, is given away in small quantities as food relief and for food for work and other aid projects or, a subject of some interest here, it is redistributed to some developing countries on a variety of gift or soft-loan terms as an import subsidy. This grain is given to countries which would otherwise have to pay cash for it, where it is seen to be in the interest of the donor nation to support their economy. Contrary to a common public view, the larger recipients of such beneficence are not the poorer developing countries, but in recent history such countries as South Korea, Israel, and Egypt.

There are a number of countries, many in Africa, in which, as the jargon has it, there is a 'structural deficit' of food i.e. an inevitable requirement to import food in any year, whether local production is good or bad. Clearly, some countries do have an inbuilt 'structural deficit'; in terms of food production, a country is a rather arbitrary concept. For example, Singapore or Hong

Kong would have obvious difficulty in feeding themselves without imports. For others, including many of the poorest countries in Africa, the concept of 'structural deficit' is less straightforward. The assumption is often made that these countries have reached a limit of food production, and that production may actually be in decline from drought and the erosion of land. The question is whether this assumption is correct, and if so whether it represents an inevitable state of affairs.

In agricultural terms Africa is enormously diverse. It is a fact that in some areas, such as the Sahel, arable production has fallen because of drought. Perhaps the best attempt to answer this question is to develop some basic principles and give one example. The basic elements of the argument are the same in all places.

In any area the limit to food production is a function of the availability of land, water, and labour, and also of three other closely linked factors—energy, or more exactly power, technology, and economics. The agriculture of Europe is now enormously productive partly because of the natural advantages of good soils, water, and a temperate and predictable climate. However, the main reason is the application of other factors. These include the controlled application of power through mechanization, other technology (improved seeds, nitrogen fertilizer, pesticides), and an economic structure which makes it worthwhile and possible for an educated farmer to use them.

Our constant lament is that we have developed a farm economy which is so successful that we seem unable to manage it without the vast overproduction of any commodity to which we direct our subsidies. Not only has production risen to an extraordinary extent, but it has become predictable within narrow limits. With rare exceptions, a farmer who sows will reap a harvest almost independent of the hazards of weather and pests. So central to European and North American politics and the taxation and expectations of the private citizen has this become—the value-added tax, the Common Agricultural Policy of the EC, and the current negotiations of the General Agreement on Tariffs and Trade (GATT)—that we may lose sight of the formidable technological achievement that it represents. Perhaps we also recoil from our success because of the public fears which have been raised by the use of technology within inadequate political and economic structures—pesticide residues and the loss of hedgerows and wildlife—which suggest that we should not inflict this technology on the developing countries. In 'development', there has perhaps been a tendency to assume that Africa and Asia should learn from the mistakes of the West and continue to use only land, water, and labour in a 'traditional' way.

We can take cereal production in highland Ethiopia as an example. This is not intended to be typical—most of Africa is not highland—but it might be fair to say that it is neither the worst nor the best case and it is consistent with our examples of famine. Highland agriculture is a 'cold' agriculture and not potentially the most productive, communications are poor and, in most of the area, no modern inputs of any kind are used. It also happens that the highland Ethiopian barley yield is almost exactly the same as United Kingdom wheat production at the time of Malthus (Hudson 1992).

The Ethiopian farmer growing barley at an altitude of 3000 metres can expect a return of around 1 ton per hectare. There is some variation in this yield—it will be less if the land is inadequately ploughed, as is the case with poorer families who cannot afford oxen. Few farmers would grow much more than a ton per hectare, and there is the ever-present risk of the loss of crops to pests and drought. By comparison, since the time of Malthus, yields per area in the UK have increased by a factor of about six. Statistics for wheat (Ministry of Agriculture, Fisheries and Food, personal communication) show an increase from about 17 bushels per acre in 1740 to an average of rather over 100 bushels per acre in 1992. Many farmers exceed that average.

The potential for an equivalent agricultural revolution in highland Ethiopia is, for reasons of terrain and absolute rainfall, rather less. However, it is entirely reasonable to suppose that if the Ethiopian farmer could obtain access to even modest technological improvements—a little phosphate, cement to improve storage and reduce losses due to rats and other pests, reliable access to pesticides, grass seed, and possibly some minor mechanization—yields could easily be doubled, and there is no reason to suppose that yields could not rise well beyond this. The 'overpopulation' of Ethiopia is relative only to the technology in use; compared with the UK, Ethiopia is almost an underpopulated country.

We can also bring in here the question of environment. The land of highland Ethiopia is disastrously over-used and eroded. Indeed, it has become almost obligatory to cite the millions of tons of highland topsoil washed down the Blue Nile each year in discussions on soil conservation. Farmers have no choice but to extend the area of cultivation to the maximum, and at the extreme farmers will now plant sheer hillsides by hand. One obvious benefit of an improved rate of production per area would be the possibility that the land area under cultivation could be reduced for an improved return. There is no technical necessity to extend land use to a maximum profit. Under the European subsidy structure, it is often an economic necessity for Western farmers who can only service debt and operate in profit by minimizing human labour and extending the cultivated area with ever more powerful and exotic machinery.

The question here is why this technology has not become available in Ethiopia. This is partly the product of circumstances—Ethiopia has suffered a protracted and disastrous civil war—but fundamentally it can be argued that it is a product of international economics. The fact is not that it cannot be done—there is no fundamental technological impediment to improving road access to rural Ethiopia, terracing the land, cementing walls and stores, applying phosphate, or even potentially replacing oxen with light machinery. The Ethiopian Government has had such plans for years and, at least in the central plateau, has made some progress. The fundamental problem is that it is not worth doing.

This is because Ethiopian cereals produced by 'traditional' methods cost more than subsidized imported grain. Although it would be technically possible to increase food production, any country which needs to import farm inputs must find hard currency to pay for them. Through the farm subsidies of the industrialized countries Ethiopian farmers are in direct competition with their European and North American counterparts. At prevailing grain prices it does not make good sense to grow more, at least in the most vulnerable and inaccessible areas. The case is not an isolated one. The Gambian or Senegalese rice farmer competes with the rice farmer of Southeast Asia and the USA but does not enjoy the advantages of infrastructure and access to inputs. The Sudan, which has an extensively developed commercial rain-fed sector, produces around a million tonnes of sorghum surplus to its own requirements in a good year (there is large variation in rainfall between years). However, direct costing in the mid-1980s showed that Sudanese sorghum cost about double the price of insured high quality wheat imported through Port Sudan, a short drive from the major surplus-producing areas.

A well-known quotation from Swift's *Gulliver's Travels* remains apt: 'Whoever could make two ears of corn or two blades of grass grow where only one grew before, would deserve better of mankind, and do more essential service to his country than the whole race of politicians put together'.

For completeness, it should be added that the case is complex, and that if some device could be found to raise farm prices there would be other effects, not least a rise in price for the poor in urban areas where jobs and investment are scarce. However, at this stage we can reach several conclusions.

Firstly, the occurrence of famine has little or nothing to do with 'food shortage'. Secondly, the evidence is that famine has become rarer in step with economic development. Thirdly, global food supplies are not short. Quite the reverse—even if there were no increase in production, there would be no reason to suppose that there would be an absolute failure of supply relative to need in the immediate future. Lastly, there is no technological impediment to a dramatic increase in food supply in many countries and every reason to believe that, in some instances at least, this would relieve rather than impose more pressure on the environment. There is every reason to believe that, if we were better organized, we could accommodate even the worst population scenario. If Malthus's positive checks occur— if areas of the world become absolutely short of food—it is because we have brought it upon ourselves, and for no other compelling reason.

FOOD SUPPLY, AGRICULTURE, AND POPULATION GROWTH

To conclude our argument we should deal with the 'preventive checks' on population, i.e. people's desire to limit their family size and their access to the means to do so. Although it might be agreed that, through a combination of economic development and redistribution, any foreseeable world population might be fed, ultimately there is the risk that the argument might lead to a planet on which we might not wish to live. At the theoretical limit, the carrying capacity of the planet is not even set by agriculture. There is no particular reason to suppose that we could not feed ourselves by producing food from primary chemical sources, leaving energy supply as the only consideration. It has been calculated that the maximum supportable population of the planet is that at which heat can no longer be radiated away, at which stage the entire planet would be covered several layers deep with human habitation. More realistically, we are less likely to secure the co-operation of the industrialized nations if the promise is of a diet of barley and mutton, and where a 'Big Mac' is only for the very rich. It would obviously be better to consider the argument in the context of stabilizing our rising world population.

I shall summarize this argument briefly, partly because it goes rather further than my subject really allows, and partly because the science of population prediction is still highly problematic. In the predictive sense, we still do not really know why people do and do not choose to limit their family size. We can ask two kinds of question. Are people more likely to choose to limit their families under conditions of plenty or of want? Under what conditions are they most likely to be able to exercise that choice?

The desire to have a family of any given size and the absolute and projected size of a population is a complex function of many factors: educational level; the age at marriage; religious belief; the current and anticipated economic situation and the relationship of the individual to it; the expectations of the wider social group; the chances of children surviving; the age and sex structure of the population concerned. At the level of the poor Ethiopian highland farmer there may still be greater advantage in having more children than less. It is true that more children will mean more mouths to feed; in the absence of many livestock to be tended they represent only a marginal return in the form of labour, and there is little chance that older children can settle locally as there is no land. However, a child migrating to an urban area to work as a labourer may remit money or grain to the family. A richer rural family with some education—particularly where the wife is educated—is likely to have fewer children, if for no other reason than that an educated woman will probably insist on a degree of spacing of pregnancies and hire labour from the numerous poor. At the other extreme, for example the middle class in the UK, the costs of children (considerable), the benefits (largely social), the generally high educational levels, and easy access to contraception all contribute to the tendency for small average families. In a very summary way, we can state that the decision is not one of absolute wealth but of circumstances. Circumstances may tend in general to favour small families in richer places, but there are many poor people in developing countries who would now choose to limit family size if they could.

In most developing countries, the demand for effective modern contraception vastly exceeds the supply. The reason that poor people in many poor countries cannot obtain contraceptives varies from country to country, but in many is fundamentally economic. Distribution of modern contraceptives requires a system. Apart from condoms, which are unpopular and comparatively unimportant as a method of contraception, modern contraceptives are used by women, and it is neither possible nor ethical to consider the use of most methods of contraception except where they are delivered as part of a health system. The poverty of many developing countries is now so extreme that services often exist only in name—for all practical purpose there are no health services at all. Government expenditure on health services in the poorer developing countries is now typically of the order of £1 per person per year.

In conclusion, it is clear that our dilemma is fundamentally economic and political. If we wish to move to a world with a stable, adequately fed population and a sustainable environment, we must first look to world economics. If we see the problem purely in terms of population control, we may indeed be on the threshold of the Malthusian famine.

REFERENCES

Daily, G. C. and Erlich, P. R. (1990). An exploratory model of the impact of rapid climate change on the world food situation. *Proceedings of the Royal Society of London*, Series B, **241**, 232–44.

Erlich, P. R. (1971). *The population bomb*. Ballantyne, London.

Hudson, P. (1992). *The industrial revolution*. Arnold, London.

Malthus T. (1982). *An essay on the principle of population*. Penguin, London. (Originally published in 1798).

UN Population Fund (1992). *State of world population 1992*. UNFPA, New York.

3

An abundance of cheap eggs, fish, and meat: the consequences

Richard Lacey

Professor Richard Lacey, MD, PhD, FRCPath, has been Professor of Medical Microbiology at the University of Leeds since 1983. After completing his medical training at Cambridge University, he was appointed Registrar at the Bristol Royal Infirmary in 1967. In the following year he was appointed to a Lectureship, and subsequently to the Readership, in Clinical Microbiology at the University of Bristol. In 1974 Professor Lacey moved to East Anglia where, as well as working as a consultant in both microbiology and chemical pathology at the Queen Elizabeth Hospital, King's Lynn, he served as Consultant in Chemical Pathology to the East Anglian Regional Health Authority until taking up his present appointment at Leeds. He also acts as a consultant to the World Health Organization. Professor Lacey has always attached importance to combining his academic and research work with continuing medical practice in the National Health Service; his experience of operating an NHS clinic in Leeds interacts with his main research interest, the health risks associated with mass-produced food.

Professor Lacey became a controversial figure, and the target of lively hostility from the farming community, in the context of the debate which followed the statement by Mrs Edwina Currie, then Minister of Health, on 3 December 1988 that 'most British egg production is infected with Salmonella'. On that occasion and in subsequent 'scares' over listeria and bovine spongiform encephalopathy (BSE), Professor Lacey has consistently argued for greater openness and against complacency.

INTRODUCTION

The populations of the developed world have become accustomed to a plentiful supply of meat and eggs, and also often fish. The real cost of these foods to the consumer has fallen typically by two- to fourfold over the last three decades. Despite the continued migration of people from rural communities to the cities, the availability of these foods, either whole or processed, has been maintained through bulk transport, now often refrigerated, and large holding stores and supermarkets on the periphery of towns and cities.

Until recently, the urban dweller rarely considered how his or her food was produced, or indeed what effect contemporary farming practices might produce on the environment. The urban dweller has succeeded in dissociating the food on the plate—or increasingly held in the fingers—from the conditions of rearing and slaughter of the animals, birds, and fish from which it is derived.

Cheap plentiful meat has seemingly been the unchallenged goal of governments, consumers, and retailers for many years, and has been achieved through the search for ever increasing *efficiency*. In farming, efficiency has come to mean the achievement of the most rapid production of meat or fish, with the optimum utilization of feedstuffs, within the smallest space. Such intensive rearing is seen most disturbingly with broilers, turkeys, pigs, and battery egg layers.

The consumer's attitude to purchasing items in supermarkets appears to be most influenced by two factors: firstly, the appearance of the product, which accounts for the ludicrous volume of packaging; and secondly, the price. Supermarket chains respond to the consumer's demand for cheap meat, fish, and eggs by applying powerful downward pressure on prices paid to the farmer. If the farmer fails to deliver the goods sufficiently cheaply, the supermarket seeks bulk produce from overseas. The problem in the UK is now acute because of the inadequacy of space for lowland farming for non-intensive food production. The exhaustion of the fishing grounds in the relatively shallow North-eastern Atlantic waters is a further problem.

Thus for some years the scene has been set for gathering crises in our food provision. However, it was probably not until one late November Saturday in 1988 when Edwina Currie, then

Junior Minister at the Department of Health, remarked that most of our egg production was contaminated with Salmonella, that there was a national awareness of the problems associated with contemporary food production. These can be summarized as follows:

- cruelty to animals, birds, and probably fish;
- environmental pollution;
- loss of some essential nutrients;
- poor flavour;
- contamination.

In considering each of these problems, the depth of the discussion will tend to reflect the interest and responsibilities of the author, and it is hoped that those incensed about revelations over cruelty, for example, will forgive its relatively brief mention.

CRUELTY

Typical methods of producing broilers provide a clear illustration of this problem. A single shed can harbour as many as 40 000 birds. These will be delivered as newborn chicks and will be kept on the floor for about seven weeks, by which time each bird will hardly be able to move. As many as 10 per cent may die, and the rotting corpses will be pecked at by those still alive until they are removed. Death can be due to infection, bone deformity, or heart failure. Each batch of broilers is referred to as a 'crop' and the tons of manure and rotting carcasses have somehow to be disposed of (Lacey 1991). The author has seen mounds of this material dumped on local agricultural land. However, by the time the broilers have been slaughtered, plucked, dressed, packaged, and arranged neatly in rows, the consumer is quite unable to associate their new image with their origins.

Many of these comments also apply to turkeys, except that cruelty may be even worse than with broilers. Firstly, the bird has become so grotesque through selective breeding that it cannot mate spontaneously and hence artificial insemination of the breeding flocks is necessary. Secondly, there appears to be a horrible preoccupation with size for its own sake. The cramped conditions must be truly 'sardine-like'.

Most people are now familiar with the battery system of egg-laying. Several chickens are housed in tiny wire cages with sloping mesh floors. After the egg is laid it rolls to a collecting gully to avoid being trodden on. Inside the cage, the only entertainment available for the chicken is pecking and defeathering its neighbours. To stop this, beaks may have to be amputated. A continuous supply of meal and water and artificial cyclical lighting complete the picture. The chicken lays its eggs daily for about 40 weeks after which it is exhausted; it is then culled and used for soups, pies, and other food processing.

Ducks are also increasingly being reared intensively, and the concern over pigs chained into tiny cubicles and veal calves kept in what are essentially tiny boxes is growing. Deer, too, are disappearing from fields and woods into sheds, and even some game birds, such as pheasants, are, initially intensively reared.

However, there are some reasons for optimism. One UK supermarket chain is offering free-range chickens and turkeys and some pigs are returning to the countryside. However, egg-layers are rarely free-range in the real sense. Barn eggs are laid by chickens enclosed in crowded conditions on the floors of large sheds, but with nesting boxes and perches. Some so-called free-range eggs are laid by chickens housed on shed floors with access to a small pen. Many do not seem to make the effort to leave the shed.

ENVIRONMENTAL PROBLEMS

It must be fairly obvious that a large heap of rotting chicken carcasses and manure can pollute the environment in various ways. Firstly, nitrates formed from bacterial activity can leach into local water supplies. Secondly, insect vectors, rodents, and indeed dust are capable of disseminating dangerous bacteria (e.g. Salmonella—see below) over long distances.

Because of the need to use organophosphorus insecticides to eliminate sea-lice from farmed salmon, this type of fish farming can damage adjacent marine life. Sometimes the pink dyes (canthaxanthin or astaxanthin) needed to colour the farmed salmon also colour other sea creatures nearby! Perhaps the most disturbing feature of salmon farming is that as it has expanded in Scotland and Ireland, so the number of wild fish in our rivers has declined. It is probable that diseased farmed salmon escape from time to time, and contaminate and destroy the wild species.

INTENSIVE FARMING AND FOOD PROCESSING: IMPLICATIONS FOR POLYUNSATURATED FATS.

There is now substantial evidence that the amount and type of fatty acids in animals, birds, and fish is determined by the nature of their diet, and indeed by other rearing conditions. Because of the conversions of many farming systems from 'free-range' to intensive over the last few decades, the fatty acid profile of our food has altered as the intensively reared animals and fish are fed novel diets. These changes cannot be expected to be confined to macroscopic fat. It follows from this that recommended diets may not now reflect the anticipated fatty acid composition, particularly that of *n*-3 polyunsaturated fatty acids (PUFAs).

Farmed fish

Fish are an excellent source of Ω-3 (*n*-3) PUFAs including linolenic acid (LN). The major *n*-3 PUFAs in phytoplankton, the fundamental diet of marine life, are eicosapentaenoic acid (EPA) and docosahexaenoic acid (DHA), and most marine wildlife will eventually become enriched with these (Denton and Lacey 1991). The major PUFA in typical Western diets is linoleic acid (LA), an *n*-6 PUFA found in many vegetable and seed oils. In humans, LA is desaturated and elongated to arachidonic acid (AA) by further metabolic conversion.

Interest in the role of *n*-3 PUFAs in human disease was first aroused by the observation that Eskimos, with diets consisting mainly of marine life, had a low incidence of atherosclerotic disease in comparison with those consuming typical Western diets (Kromann and Green 1980). Further studies have supported the view that diets rich in *n*-3 PUFAs are effective in reducing the incidence of subsequent coronary artery disease. Consumption of fish oils in man leads to the accumulation of EPA and DHA in plasma and platelet and tissue phospholipids at the expense of AA. This change appears to have a number of biochemical and physiological effects. There is a reduction in plasma triglyceride levels and effects on total plasma cholesterol and high density lipoprotein cholesterol. There is a marked reduction in platelet aggregation associated with a lengthened bleeding time and an increase in erythrocyte deformability (Denton and Lacey 1991).

As fishing grounds have become depleted, there has been an increase in the production of farm-reared fish for human consumption. Such fish will be fed artificial feeds. As with mammals, the fatty acid content of fish can be substantially altered by making changes to their diet. Commercial fish feeds appear to contain less *n*-3 PUFAs and more *n*-6 PUFAs than natural fish diets. For example, feeds for farmed salmon can contain 10 per cent beef liver or 25 per cent cereals. There is a reduction of 15–33 per cent in the *n*-3 PUFA content and an increase of 50–100 per cent in the *n*-6 PUFA content in farmed salmon flesh compared with that of their wild counterparts (Agren *et al.* 1987). Farm-reared fish also have up to 50 per cent more total lipid fat content expressed per gram of flesh.

The effect that these changes may have on the desirable biochemical and physiological properties of these fish, when consumed, has not been studied in clinical trials. However, it is known that coronary artery atherosclerosis runs a more rapid course in farmed salmon than in wild salmon (Saunders and

Farrell 1988). It must be concluded that fish oils derived from farmed salmon, and possibly other fish, may not produce the beneficial effects in man seen with those from wild fish. Further research is needed in this area.

Chickens and eggs

In the UK, chicken meat comprises the greatest single source of meat and about 30 million eggs are consumed daily. One factor responsible for the popularity of chicken meat was the advice given in 1976 by the Royal College of Physicians of London and the British Cardiac Society (Royal College 1976) that chicken meat, being low in fat, was preferable to red meat. However, Crawford and Marsh (1989) have pointed out that at the end of the last century the carcass fat on chicken was of the order of 2.4 per cent (by weight), but it had risen to 22 per cent by the early 1980s—evidently much greater than that in some red meats. The amount and nature of fatty acids in chicken meat is influenced by the diet and rearing conditions. Such variables include the degree of unsaturation of the dietary fatty acids, the proportion of *cis* to *trans* isomers, the amount of biotin, and the temperature of rearing.

The relationship between dietary fatty acids and their concentration in tissues may not correlate closely because there is evidence of synthesis *de novo* of some fatty acids, and even unsaturated acids, in chicken tissues. However, the following diets rich in Ω-3 fatty acids, particularly α-LN, appear to result in enhanced deposition of such fatty acids in chicken tissues: corn oil and partially hydrogenated soybean oil, linseed, menhaden and natural soybean oil, canola, flax oil, and redfish oil (Hulan *et al.* 1988; Denton and Lacey 1991). In these experiments control diets were rich in barley, wheat, spent restaurant grease, or chicken fat itself.

The composition of the fatty acids in egg yolks is also markedly influenced by the diet of the laying chicken. Simopoulos and Salem (1989) have compared the effect of rearing laying chickens on a diet rich in the plant purslane with a 'standard' diet that yielded 'supermarket' eggs. Purslane is claimed to be the richest source of *n*-3 fatty acids of any green leafy vegetable (Simopoulos and Salem 1986). The average total *n*-3 fatty acid content of the 'supermarket' eggs was 1.73 mg/g and that in the Greek purslane-fed eggs was 17.66 mg/g. The corresponding figures for α-LN were 0.52 mg/g and 6.9 mg/g.

Cattle

In 1968, Crawford reported that the nature of fatty acids varied dramatically between animals reared under free-living and domestic conditions: notably, the percentage content of total weight of wild buffalo fat was 2.8 per cent, whereas that of domestic cattle (i.e. butcher's meat) was 25.0 per cent (Crawford 1968). Within the total fat, the proportions of polyunsaturated to monosaturated and saturated fatty acids were also variable: just 2.2 per cent of the fatty acids in domestic beef were polyunsaturated, but in buffalo between 10 and 30 per cent were polyunsaturated according to herd. The lower figure was from animals confined to open parkland and the higher from animals in woodland. In recent years, the effect of different cattle diets on milk and meat have been studied under experimental conditions, and generally the variations are much less than with chickens. The main reason for this is the bacterial activity within the rumen that tends to convert any dietary fat towards saturation. White *et al.* (1987) showed that, following a diet enriched by sunflower seeds, the rumen of Holstein steers decreased the amount of LA and increased that of the saturated stearic and palmitic acids. Work in France has shown that this change in the rumen is due directly to hydrogenation (Doreau *et al.* 1989). Thus when lactating cows are fed diets high in unsaturated oils, the increase in unsaturated fat in milk is small.

Pigs

In their natural state pigs roam and forage in forests. In medieval times, peasants controlled wild pigs and fed them mainly acorns in winter. These are rich in LA, and pigs fed in this way would be expected to have a ratio of polyunsaturated to saturated fatty acids of 2 : 1. In contrast, the ratio for the modern pig is reversed to 0.2 : 1 (Crawford and Marsh 1989).

The relationship between the fatty acid content of the pig's feed and that of the animal's carcass is well understood. For example, Rammell *et al.* (1988) studied the effect of a chemically defined diet on various organs of the pig. The proportion of polyunsaturated to total fatty acids was 38 per cent in the feed, 36 per cent in serum, and 39 per cent in liver.

Feeding pigs supplements of sunflower oil produces softer and oilier carcase fat and dramatically increases (by about 75 per cent) the proportion of polyunsaturated to saturated fatty acid in both muscle and adipose tissue (Rhee *et al.* 1988). Indeed, the flavour of the meat, in addition to the biochemical parameters, is influenced by the nature of the pig's diet. Thus, while canola oil is effective in increasing the carcass content of PUFAs, it produces meat with a greater tendency to 'off flavours' (Miller *et al.* 1990). These authors fed pigs a control diet of corn and soybean meal and test diets containing 10 per cent animal fat, safflower oil, sunflower oil, or canola oil. The pigs were slaughtered after 90 days at 100 kg weight. There were no obvious differences in growth with each regime, except that there was somewhat more fat with each of the fat supplements. All the oils increased the proportion of oleic acid and reduced that of palmitic acid.

FOOD POISONING AND FOOD-BORNE INFECTION

General

Even if we take the most pessimistic figures, the chances of any one person suffering from food poisoning in any year is no greater than 1 in 50. This explains why many commentators claim there is no problem—they themselves have not succumbed! The reason for the recent concern has been the upward trend in the number of cases in the UK over the last five years. The trend for other infectious diseases, even AIDS, is in the opposite direction—downwards, or at least level. Therefore food poisoning is a real problem. The figures for Campylobacter, Shigella, and Salmonella in West Leeds are shown in Fig. 3.1. The nature of the specimens from patients, the catchment area of the patients, and the laboratory methods were unchanged between 1984 and 1992. The trend in the incidence of food poisoning and gastroenteritis is depressingly upwards.

Food poisoning in the strict sense results from eating bacterial toxins, notably *Clostridium botulinum*, *Clostridium perfringens*, *Staphylococcus aureus*, and *Bacilus cereus*. Salmonella poisoning results from the formation of the enterotoxin, mainly in the intestine. Strictly speaking, *Campylobacter* spp., *Listeria*

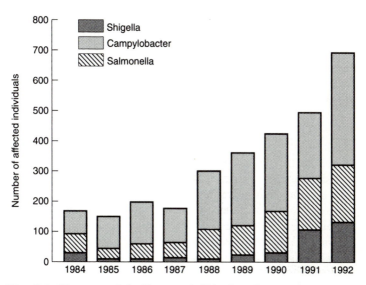

Fig. 3.1. The annual incidence of Shigella, Campylobacter, and Salmonella in West Leeds.

monocytogenes, *Vibrio parahaemolyticus* (the Japanese raw fish problem), and small bowel viruses are sources of food-borne infections since they cause disease only after multiplication to large numbers in the bowel. However, it seems sensible to group all these pathogens into one food-poisoning class. Nearly all the above micro-organisms are widely distributed, and many people will eat them from time to time with no harm. Illness from these bacteria results from the occurrence of certain factors that render the microbe dangerous in the particular item of food. In addition, host factors will determine the severity of the resultant poisoning. The natural source of these agents and their potential spread to other foods is summarized in Table 3.1.

Salmonella food poisoning is probably the best known, and the high prevalence of *Salmonella enteritidis* in recent years has enabled us to be certain for the first time that eggs and poultry really are its main source. Previously *Salmonella typhimurium* was the commonest strain, but was associated with many birds and mammals. Of the food-poisoning incidents directly attributable to *S. enteritidis* in the UK, it is likely that around 70 per cent are due to eggs and 30 per cent are due to chicken meat. *S. enteritidis* is probably a world-wide problem, and its origin is considered later in the chapter.

Chicken meat is usually contaminated with Salmonella during the automated decapitation, plucking, and evisceration of the broilers. This also appears to be the explanation for the widespread contamination of chicken meat with Campylobacter, which so far has not appeared to affect eggs.

The key to understanding *Listeria monocytogenes* is that this bacterium is fairly resistant to heating, and so cooking may only stun it rather than eliminate it from the food. If cooked food is then kept cold, even at temperatures as low as 0°C, the bacterium can recover after a few days and then multiply. When growing at low temperatures, *L. monocytogenes* produces an abundance of a toxin that reduces the ability of the human macrophage to dissolve the bacteria. Fortunately, most people have fairly good natural reistance to *L. monocytogenes*, since once it is established the resultant meningitis and/or septicaemia can be severe, with the risk of transplacental spread in pregnant women.

Food poisoning due to *Bacillus cereus* is relatively straight-forward: it results from contamination of boiled rice with spores that germinate if the rice is kept at room temperature for too long. The unsuspecting customer of the takeaway may think that his or her fried rice has been freshly cooked, whereas more probably a portion of boiled rice will have been warmed briefly in a frying pan!

The two clostridial causes of food poisoning require an absence of oxygen in the food and the presence of moisture and nutrients. Staphylococcal poisoning results from the chance inoculation of food with strains that just happen to produce a powerful poison, still described as an enterotoxin, that in fact acts centrally. The main clinical features are shown in Table 3.1.

Most food-poisoning bacteria and their toxins have no taste or smell. The smell of putrefaction is usually due to relatively harmless pseudomonads. Hence we cannot identify whether a particular food is contaminated at the point of eating. Therefore the science of food hygiene is calculated to avoid the presence of these contaminants.

Management of food poisoning

Ideally, all patients with gastrointestinal and other symptoms which might be attributable to food poisoning should be investigated thoroughly. However, this requires more resources than are available. The actual approach must have the following aims:

- identify the scale of the problem of food poisoning;
- make specific diagnoses in individual patients;
- initiate investigation into the identity of contaminated food.

Fortunately, major outbreaks are rare. When several patients present simultaneously with suspected food poisoning, referral of faecal samples, possible vomit, and available food to the

Table 3.1 Food-poisoning bacteria

Agent	Natural source	Other food or drink vectors	Incubation period
Salmonella spp.	Chickens, eggs, ducks, turkeys	Many prepared foods, notably cooked meats, bean sprouts	18 hours–2 days
Campylobacter spp.	Poultry meat, unpasteurized milk	Water	5–7 days
Listeria monocytogenes	Soil, animal manure, water	Chilled and processed foods, soft-crusted cheeses, cooked chicken, pâté, salamis, recipe (cook – chill) meals, salads	5 days– 5 weeks
Bacillus cereus	Widely in environment	Take-away fried rice	6–18 hours
Clostridium botulinum	Soil, vegetables, fish	Defective canned items of vegetables or fish, processed meat and vegetables	12–18 hours
Clostridium perfringens	Intestines of mammals including man	Stews, minces, anaerobic food	12–24 hours
Staphylococcus aureus	Noses, groins, intestines of mammals including man, birds	Cream, cooked meats, custards, moist processed foods	1–3 hours

Typical patient	Symptoms and signs	Estimated no. of cases (UK 1992)	Estimated no. of deaths (UK 1992)
Anyone, particularly the very young and old	Diarrhoea, abdominal pains	300 000	100
Particularly young healthy adults, immunity can develop	Bloody diarrhoea, abdominal pain, exhaustion	350 000	1
Pregnant women, elderly immuno-compromised, also some young healthy adults	Influenza-like illness in pregnancy, stillbirth, septicaemia, meningitis, few gut symptoms	400	100
Anyone	Diarrhoea, abdominal pain	1000	0
Anyone	Progressive paralysis of motor nerves	0	0
Anyone	Diarrhoea, abdominal pain	5000	0
Anyone	Vomiting, sometimes severe with haematemesis	5000	5

Based on the official number of cases reported up to end November 1992 to the Government's Communicable Disease Surveillance Centre, multiplied by factors (e.g. 10 for Salmonella, 3 for Listeria) to allow for inefficient reporting.

laboratory is mandatory. Notification of the incident to the appropriate officers is essential and will initiate a probe into the circumstances. It is important that the patients do not warn a suspected caterer of imminent scrutiny!

The question of when to investigate sporadic cases is much harder, and depends on local facilities.

Although water is not strictly a food, we must be alert to the possibility of epidemics of diarrhoea due to the protozoan parasite *Cryptosporidium*. This is well known in AIDS patients, but may also occur in otherwise healthy patients, especially children. Although there is no treatment, it is worth attempting to identify the parasite in faeces. This enables the outbreak to be traced back to defective sand filtering from the reservoirs.

Treatment

Most food poisoning results in loss of water and electrolytes, with a risk of hypovolaemia (i.e. shock) and possible rare vascular complications in the acute phase. Fruit juices are the mainstay of treatment. Antibiotics have little role, even against Campylobacter, which is sensitive to erythromycin, because this is a self-limiting infection and clinical trials have not shown benefit. Antidiarrhoeal drugs such as codeine and loperamide are rarely contraindicated. The great majority of cases can be managed at home. However, the 1–2 per cent of patients with microbiological complications of Salmonella food poisoning may require treatment in hospital for septicaemia and abscesses. Antibiotics for these include co-trimoxazole or trimethoprim, chloramphenicol, or ampicillin. Quinolones such as ciprofloxacin may be effective, but should be used sparingly because of the risk of selection of resistance.

The incidence of prolonged Salmonella carriage must have increased recently, and for the great majority of patients it is emphatically not warranted to send serial specimens to the laboratory to satisfy our curiosity as to when the pathogen has gone! Most people should return to normal activities with the disappearance of the diarrhoea, with instructions for meticulous personal hygiene. A few patients who work in health care or catering may need specific management—it is suggested that this is discussed with their employers and if necessary the Medical Officer for Environmental Health or the equivalent. Even with these people there is a trend towards a less aggressive attitude over staying away from work until the Salmonella has disappeared. There is a suspicion that quinolone antibiotics might reduce the length of carriage. However, more data are required.

Listeriosis

The management of patients with suspected listeriosis, particularly in pregnancy, depends principally on blood culture analysis. *L. monocytogenes* grows readily on simple laboratory media. The differential diagnosis of an influenza-like illness in pregnancy includes actual virus infections, urinary infections, and listeriosis. If possible, any products from miscarriages should be sent to the laboratory for culture. Although listeriosis is not common, the establishment of a link with any particular food is difficult because of the long interval between diagnosis of illness and eating the food, and so any information is valuable.

In summary, food poisoning is a costly and complicated medical problem. It is multifactorial and on the increase. Contamination of food at source remains the major cause.

THE PROBLEM OF SALMONELLA IN EGGS

The recent dramatic increase in Salmonella cannot be accounted for by any of the following explanations:

- change of isolating and reporting procedures;
- change of vulnerability of the patient or pathogenicity of the bacterium;
- major changes in kitchen hygiene or catering practice;
- the occurrence of one or a few large outbreaks which

Richard Lacey

artificially 'inflate' the figures—indeed, *the number of such incidents has recently declined.*

Similarly, there has been a decline in the last few years of hospital Salmonella outbreaks associated with catering errors. This suggests that hygiene control may be improving, perhaps due to publicity and the Food Act of 1990. It is an inescapable conclusion that eggs are the source of the additional contamination that has led to the increase in Salmonella poisoning.

Many species of Salmonella, notably *S. typhimurium* and *S. enteritidis*, have been associated with poultry and eggs for many years. There has been an acceptance that the contamination of eggshells by droppings, associated with washing and cracking, can implant small numbers of Salmonellae into the egg albumen. This problem has been containable for the following reasons.

1. The egg white is relatively hostile to the multiplication of Salmonella owing to the presence of inhibitory substances, including lysozyme.
2. Eggs are now rarely washed in the UK.
3. Battery-produced eggs permit the ready removal of droppings through the wire floors with gentle rolling of the laid eggs for collection.

Salmonella enteritidis

The major change in the epidemiology of Salmonella poisoning concerns the increase in *S. enteritidis*, the source of which is essentially poultry (Humphrey *et al.* 1988). Between 1982 and 1987 the number of reported cases of *S. enteritidis* food poisoning in England and Wales increased sixfold from 1101 to 6858 (*Lancet* 1988). During this time, notifications of Salmonella other than *S. enteritidis* have remained fairly constant (*Communicable Disease Reports* 1982–8).

S. enteritidis type 4 has rarely been associated with foods other than those containing chicken or egg ingredients. It is certainly likely that the source of some of the food poisoning from *S. enteritidis* is chicken meat, but there would appear to be no reason for such an increase in this. No data have been presented showing that contamination of chicken meat by Salmonella has increased recently. Furthermore, the contamination is usually 'light', and 'normal' cooking should destroy salmonellae associated with surfaces of chicken. However, it is accepted that some *S. enteritidis* type 4 may be derived from chicken meat rather than eggs. It also follows that other *S. enteritidis* types and *S. typhimurium* may also contribute to egg-derived food poisoning.

It is often difficult to establish the cause of food poisoning because, whilst the bacteria can be isolated from the patient, the remains of the food responsible may have been discarded. Eggs present a particular problem because individual eggs are unlabelled, making tracing the source difficult. The egg, particularly the yolk, may have been completely consumed, and there is often no yolk adhering to the inside of the shell after cracking.

Despite these problems, the association between *S. enteritidis* type 4 (and some other types), food poisoning, and eggs is well established (Coyle *et al.* 1988; Perales and Audicana 1988; St. Louis *et al.* 1988).

Salmonella enteritidis type 4 in the internal organs of laying birds and in eggs

Three independent reports have shown that *S. enteritidis* type 4 is present in a high percentage of the internal organs of laying birds, including the ovaries and oviducts (Hopper and Mawer 1988; Lister 1988; O'Brien 1988). The findings of Hopper and Mawer are particularly significant. These authors state 'despite the evident presence of *S. enteritidis* type 4 infection in this flock of 60 000 birds, mortality and egg production have remained at expected levels' (Hopper and Mawer 1988). They studied the liver, caecum, oviduct, and ovule of 50 birds and found that 13 (26 per cent) contained *S. enteritidis* type 4. A recent survey of individual eggs obtained from various sources showed that 0.6 per cent of eggs from several sources in Devon contained Salmonella (Humphrey 1992).

The evidence linking *Salmonella enteritidis* type 4 food poisoning to eggs

Given the nature of the problems discussed above, the evidence for such a link is not conclusive, but it is as strong as can be obtained. It is based partly on epidemiology and partly on direct culture of the chicken's organs and eggs. However, it is the *only* plausible explanation for the dramatic rise in *S. enteritidis* food poisoning. It is often not possible to establish a clear link in sporadic cases for the reasons given above, and it is not reasonable to expect such proof. A useful analogy may illustrate the problem. Epidemiological and experimental data have established that smoking causes lung cancer in general, although such causal proof is lacking in the individual patient who succumbs from the disease.

The scale of the problem

The numbers of reported isolations of *S. enteritidis* type 4 have been about 300 weekly over the last three years, with peaks in late summer. Whilst it is possible that not all these are derived from eggs, and some other species may also contaminate eggs, the figure of 300 reports may be taken as representative of egg-derived bacteria. The true incidence of the disease can only be arrived at by conjecture. Because our surveillance system is passive—patients fail to offer themselves for diagnosis or to provide specimens, and laboratories fail to isolate and report cases—the numbers officially presented are obviously less than the actual figures. Indeed, it is commonly stated that only 10 per cent of food poisoning incidents are reported (*Lancet* 1988). If this figure is accepted, the current incidence of *S. enteritidis* type 4 food poisoning is 150 000 per year.

The source of the problem

Food poisoning due to *S. enteritidis* type 4 is a Europe-wide problem. Eggs shown to be contaminated with this bacterium have been found in Spain, Italy, and Germany as well as the UK. The isolation of genetically identical bacteria from such a wide territory suggests either the spread of Salmonella between laying flocks, occurring on a massive scale, or the dissemination of Salmonella from a single point source. Transovarian transmission (i.e. contamination of the contents of eggs directly from the ovaries) makes the latter explanation highly plausible because almost all European laying flocks are ultimately derived from two breeding, or elite, flocks in Holland and France, and it is tempting to assume that these flocks are also contaminated with this organism. We can now make some sense of the cause of the Salmonella problems and propose the following mechanism.

As a result of recycling chicken remains (and their Salmonella) back to chickens, evolutionary pressures have forced Salmonella and chicken to exist symbiotically or commensally. This means that the salmonella can exist within the chicken without necessarily damaging it (it is evidently not in the 'interest' of a bacterium to kill its host). If this occurred in the breeding flocks, eggs hatched subsequently from these could contain Salmonella that would infect emerging chicks. These, perhaps after only a brief illness, would then harbour the Salmonella in their internal organs including their ovaries. When mature they will lay eggs, some of which would once again be contaminated with salmonella.

If this reasoning is correct, and it would seem to be the only explanation for the wide distribution of the bacteria, then the main thrust of the control of Salmonella must be to develop Salmonella-free breeding flocks. The measures taken by the government (slaughtering infected laying flocks) will not produce a long-term solution because new laying flocks will also be liable to be contaminated with salmonella.

The cost of establishing salmonella-free breeding flocks and the reduction of subsequent contamination will not be excessive, perhaps increasing the cost of an egg by 0.2–1p. Scientific ability to do this is certainly adequate at present. The presence of Salmonella in the internal organs of chickens can be detected by a blood test, a vaccine is available, and harmless bacteria can be fed to newborn chicks to compete with and prevent possible contamination by Salmonella. However, we do not seem to possess the will or organization to put this procedure into practice.

BOVINE SPONGIFORM ENCEPHALOPATHY (BSE)

The emergence of BSE must be seen as a consequence of the need for cheap protein-rich feed supplements to stimulate cattle growth. These concentrates, mainly added to winter feeds, were obtained from rendering plants that converted otherwise unwanted animal and bird remains into fat (tallow) used in cosmetics and into bone meal rich in protein. This practice has developed since the 1970s or possibly earlier, and was largely unknown to the public. Many people, with hindsight, have pointed out that it is *de facto* cannabilism when such a product is fed to the same species from which it was derived. Certainly the procedure provided an abundance of cheap protein-rich feed.

The first cases of the current epidemic of BSE occurred in 1985 and were confirmed during 1986 (Dealler and Lacey 1990). Since then the number of notified cases had risen to a total of around 75 000 by the autumn of 1993. Infected dairy cows have been reported much more often than infected beef cattle and comprise at least 95 per cent of cases, presumably because cows typically live to be six or seven years old before slaughter and beef cattle typically live between two and three years. The incubation period of this disease is not known, but the median age at death is four years seven months (Wilesmith *et al.* 1988). This explains why many cattle will be slaughtered before the infectious agent that they are carrying has had time to produce the final clinical disease.

Perhaps the most significant feature of BSE has been its wide geographical spread, involving farms in many parts of England, Wales, Scotland, Northern Ireland, Eire, and even the Isle of Man. However, a substantial number of herds have not reported any cases at all and it is by no means certain that all herds are infected. That the agent has appeared so widely and in many different breeds, and that the age of death is usually between three and five years indicate that feed was the vector for the infection (Wilesmith *et al.* 1988). This is extremely important because there has been uncertainty over the predominant means of acquisition of this group of infectious diseases (transmissible spongiform encephalopathies (TSEs)) as a whole.

Whilst the total number of diagnosed cases of around 75 000 among perhaps 10 million cows and beef cattle is an indication of the extent of the problem, the real numbers must be greater than this since many animals will be slaughtered before the time required for the clinical disease to develop fully. It is not known how many animals carry the infectious agent but never become clinically ill. The reason for this uncertainty is that virtually no research has been done in this area.

The contaminated feed was initially thought to have been used between 1981 and mid-1988 (Wilesmith *et al.* 1988), after which the feeding of rendered offal to ruminants was prohibited by the BSE Order. This feed contained protein supplements derived from rendering plants. This protein concentrate was also added to feeds for poultry, sheep, and pigs. For this reason the dissemination of the infectious agent causing BSE has been extremely widespread, although the disease has so far been manifest primarily in cows and to a lesser extent in beef cattle. One of the implications from this is that any attempt to eliminate the infection from the pastures and buildings of this country would be a truly monumental task.

The disease BSE results from a damaged brain that shows histological spongiform change and the presence of excess amounts of PrP and SAF proteins (Dealler and Lacey 1990). However, the disease agent must pass through a number of organs between its entry into the animal's body through the gut and the final multiplication in the brain (Table 3.2). Most of the work on the distribution of TSEs has been performed in sheep, and the Government seemed to rely on such evidence to identify which organs are likely to contain the infectious agent in cows. Thus the spleen, the lymphatics, the thymus, the spinal cord, and the brain have been designated high risk organs and are not permitted to enter the food chain (except from calves under 6 months). However, certain knowledge of the distribution of the infectious agent in cattle will take very

Table 3.2 Tissues containing infectious agents for TSEs

Tissue	Sheep	Goat	Mouse	Mink	Man	Cow
Brain	+	+	+	+	+	+
Spinal cord	+	+	+	+	+	
Peripheral nerve	+	+	+			
Eye					+	
Adrenal gland		+				
Lymph node	+	+	+	+		
Tonsil		+				
Salivary gland		+	+	+		
Spleen	+	+	+	+	+	
Gut	+	+	+	+		
Liver		+	+	+		
Kidney			+	+		
Bladder				+		
Lung			+	+		
Thymus			+	+		
Uterus			+			
Blood/serum				+	+	
Bone marrow			+			
Cerebrospinal fluid		+			+	
Faeces				+		
Muscle		+		+		

+ denotes presence of infectious agent. TSEs have not been detected in pancreas, heart, thyroid, testis, ovary, urine, saliva, milk, or mammary gland from one or more species. From Dealler and Lacey 1990.

many years, because the identification of each agent is still an extremely lengthy procedure. Whilst tissue proteins associated with infection, such as PrP and SAFs, are amenable to detection through tissue-staining and biochemical methods, the actual certain identification of the presence of the infectious agent can still only be made by injection into test animals such as mice. These experiments can take up to a year to be completed.

Indeed, one uncertainty about these experiments is that even if a group of mice is not infected by potentially infected material, it does not establish that there is no such material present since it could mean that the material in the donor animal has no specific affinity for mice. One of the features of these agents is that once they have moved from one host to another the *subsequent* host range can change. Thus in the natural 'experiment' in the 1950s and 1960s in North America the infective agent from sheep scrapie passed to mink, and when the agents from sheep and mink were then studied for the host range, major differences were apparent. For example, sheep scrapie had no affinity for rhesus monkeys (consistent with a view that sheep scrapie does not affect man) but the agent from mink did produce disease in this host.

This means that it is extremely difficult to prove conclusively by experiment whether or not BSE can infect humans. Of course, it is not ethical to challenge members of the human population with such infectious agents deliberately (and it is gratifying to see that the Health and Safety Executive is treating all such tissues from infective animals as suspect and requiring very careful containment facilities to be provided before any laboratory experiments). Consider, for example, the possibility of a person already infected with this agent which may, perhaps, be present in the spleen. By this time the agent may have undergone some host modification as a result of its presence in the human body for some time. If parts of that spleen are injected into mice, and if infection is subsequently induced, it establishes that the infection in the human spleen is now in a state capable of infecting mice, but it does not prove that the agent is certain to damage the human brain.

Similarly, a negative result in mice cannot guarantee that the human brain will not be involved subsequently. However, a series of experiments have been performed by workers for the UK Government (Table 3.3). At the time of writing, of seven species of mammals challenged by various routes, only hamsters have not succumbed. It is possible that their apparent immunity to this disease has resulted from their short life-span. The most disturbing experiments were performed in pigs (seven out of ten succumbed) and marmoset monkeys (two out of two). Both pig and monkey tissues have close similarities to human tissue. Whilst the inoculating material contained a high titre of infectious agent, the experiments raise the distinct possibility, or more likely probability, that man is vulnerable, although not within the time-scale of these experiments.

It is interesting that only a minority of sheep challenged were vulnerable. This is certainly consistent with the proposal that BSE originated in cattle, rather than in sheep as claimed by Southwood (1989).

During the last few years a number of animals (and one bird) have suffered from newly described spongiform encephalopathies. These include domestic cats, zoo cats (e.g. a puma), oryx, eland, and ostrich. It is probable, but not capable of proof, that contaminated bovine material was responsible.

One disquieting feature of these infectious agents is that there is no evidence of an immunological response to their presence. As a consequence, there is no serological (blood) test for their presence. This lack of immune response raises the disturbing possibility that infectivity is related directly to the total amount of agent ingested over the years, in the same way that the adverse effects of smoking or exposure to ionizing radiation are cumulative. This could mean that, because of its persistence in nervous tissue for example, the repetitive consumption of a small amount of agent in contaminated meat could well provide a danger comparable to ingestion of a large amount of brain material on a single occasion. These infectious agents have not been detected in the milk of infected mammals.

Table 3.3 Experimental transmissions of BSE to cattle and other species

Species	Number of animals challenged	Number developing an SE	Age at challenge (approx.)	Period between challenge and confirmation	Mode of infection*
Cattle	16	16	4–5 months	17–24 months	i.c., i.v.
Pigs	10	7	2 weeks	17–37 months	i.c., i.v., i.p.
Marmoset	2	2	14 months	48–49 months	i.c. i.p.
Goat	3	3	4–6 years	506–570 days	i.c.
Goat	3	1	2–5 years	941 days	Oral
Sheep	11	4	6–18 months	440–880 days	i.c.
Sheep	12	3	6–18 months	538–994 days	Oral
Mouse	2117	648	4–8 weeks	265–722 days	i.c., i.p.
Mouse	450	138	4–8 weeks	317–616 days	i.c.
Mouse	94	5	4–8 weeks	504–596 days	i.p.
Mouse	10	10	4–6 weeks	435–540 days	Oral

* i.c., intracerebral inoculation; i.v., intravenous inoculation; i.p., intraperitoneal inoculation. The material used for all these experiments was brain material from confirmed BSE cases, which is the only tissue to date that has shown any infectivity.

Nature of the infectious agent causing BSE and other spongiform encephalopathies

None of the theories relating to the identity of the infectious agent can accommodate all the known facts. Either a substantial amount of experimental work is in error or has been misinterpreted, or the actual mode of infectivity, once it has been elucidated, will reveal new insights into fundamental cellular biochemistry. Certainly, as mentioned above, a number of tissue proteins have been associated with the infectious agent. However, it is not known whether any of these is the actual infectious agent itself or the result of the infectious agent reacting with existing tissue structures or indeed in various ways promoting the formation of these substances. What is known about the pathogenesis of TSEs is that there is an infectious basis in the majority of the animals involved. The agent must be capable of securing its self-replication and there must be a means for it to spread between tissues.

It is also known that the agent is extremely small and resistant to damage by physical agents, notably heat. Persistence of some infectivity can occur after heating to 360°C for 1 hour (Brown *et al*. 1990). It is also resistant to most routinely used antiseptics and ionizing radiation. TSEs can survive for 3 years in soil. This suggests that it will be virtually impossible to eliminate these agents from our country for many decades, if not centuries.

As for the chemical composition of the agent, Prusiner (1989) suggests that it consists of a tightly packed protein known as a prion and very little else. It is known that protease K, and enzyme specific for proteins, is able to inactivate the agent. Other workers, such as the Edinburgh group, have suggested that a small piece of DNA is involved that somehow enables the infective agent to replicate. However, the presence of any DNA is difficult to reconcile with its extraordinary physical toughness.

It is worth mentioning briefly the known human diseases which are due to TSEs. Kuru was endemic in the Fore tribe in New Guinea in the early part of the century and was due to cannibalistic practices, particularly among women who tended to eat human tissue. Education has now stopped this practice. The women typically developed the disease 15–20 years after the first exposure. The main clinical features of kuru were musculoskeletal disorders rather than problems of intellect. Creutzfeldt–Jakob disease (CJD), which has been known since the early 1920s, typically occurs in middle age, and whilst perhaps 10 per cent of cases are familial, the great majority are sporadic and the main effect is seen as damage to the intellect with less evidence of musculoskeletal disorders. For this reason, many patients with CJD spend their terminal illness in mental institutions. Post mortems are rarely performed in these patients and so many cases of CJD will be missed. It has been estimated that the real number of CJD cases is of the order of 1500–9000 per year (Roberts 1990), whereas the official notification figures are about one case per million per year.

The important and unsolved questions are as follows:

1. Is BSE capable of spreading to man?
2. What is the origin of CJD?

The most pessimistic hypothesis gives the same answer to these questions: today's cases of CJD are due to consumption of the BSE agent some 20–30 years ago. This would have been before it had become amplified to the extent that it has now. Rare cases or subclinical infection in cows and beef cattle could well have been missed (Dealler and Lacey 1990).

The question of the origin of the sporadic cases of CJD suggests that the cow is the most likely source because it is the only mammal that is eaten regularly when it is elderly. Other mammals are a less probable source. There appears to be no association between sheep scrapie and CJD (Southwood 1989), and the consumption of pig products usually occurs when the animal is only five or six months old. Moreover, CJD is most prevalent in Jewish populations.

Knowledge from accidents whereby human growth hormone and various transplants have been transferred to patients and the evidence from CJD and kuru suggest that the incubation period for TSEs in humans will rarely be less than 10 years when acquired by the oral route, and could well be 40 years or more. For this reason there will be no reassurance that humans are not liable to be infected by these agents from BSE-contaminated meat until 1996 at the earliest, and probably not until the first part of the next century.

Meanwhile, there must be a massive investment into investigation of the disease and a search for chemotherapeutic agents that might modify the illness. The dilemma that our politicians face is that to undertake such a programme would admit the gravity of the problem which itself would have a devastating effect on farming and other aspects of our community. For this reason the Government has relied on hoping that the effect on humans will be minor and delayed, and has attempted to reassure members of the public by stating that BSE has the same infectivity as sheep scrapie.

Government action

The Southwood Report

In April 1988 Sir Richard Southwood was asked to set up a working party to advise on BSE. In June 1988 Southwood recommended that carcasses of affected animals should be destroyed. This was never implemented adequately in that most carcasses were dumped in land-fill sites, a most unsatisfactory procedure because of the extreme hardiness of the infective agent (Brown and Gajdusek 1991). Of course, such carcasses should be incinerated. Unfortunately, there were inadequate facilities, and little effort has been made to build new incinerators. In November 1988 Southwood recommended that the ban on the use of ruminent-based protein for ruminants should continue indefinitely.

The full text of the Southwood report was published in February 1989. The key conclusion was as follows (Southwood 1989, p.21):

From present evidence, it is likely that cattle will prove to be a 'dead-end host' for the disease agent and most unlikely that BSE will have any implications for human health. Nevertheless, if our assessments of these likelihoods are incorrect, the implications would be extremely serious.

The first statement is evidently tautological in that if cattle are indeed a dead-end host for the infectious agent, this means it will not transfer to any other host, including humans. However, the real worry with this statement is that by February 1989 insufficient time had elapsed to know whether BSE might spread spontaneously or experimentally to other mammals. *There was no evidence* as to whether or not cattle would prove a dead-end host. Since then, BSE has been successfuly transmitted to many mammals and has probably also infected cats and zoo animals such as oryx and antelopes and their offspring. Therefore, we now know that cattle are not a 'dead-end' host, and we agree fully with Southwood's conditional comment, which is now an operational statement, that 'the implications would be extremely serious'.

This has largely been ignored by much of the Ministry of Agriculture, Fisheries and Food (MAFF). In particular, ministers have continued to quote the phase that it is 'most unlikely that BSE will have any implications for human health' out of context, both literally and temporally.

The final and most decisive recommendation was 'that this [i.e. the rendering plant] method of disposing animal waste should be changed so as to eliminate these novel pathways for pathogens' (Southwood 1989).

Largely on the basis of evidence provided by MAFF veterinary advisers (Wilesmith *et al.* 1988), Southwood considered that sheep offal was the cause of BSE and that once this source of infection was removed, the numbers would plateau at 350–400 a month and then drop in the early 1990s with a total of 17 000–20 000 cases. Unfortunately, this optimism has not been vindicated by events. Using figures from parliamentary questions to MAFF the number of BSE cases each year in the UK between 1987 and 1992 were as follows:

1987	400
1988	2 200
1989	6 400
1990	13 000
1991	24 000
1992 (estimated)	39 000

The progressive rise in BSE cases must have resulted from the multiplication of the infectious agent in bovine tissues rather than in sheep, since the sheep population has only risen slightly in recent years.

How such multiplication in bovine tissues has occurred is not certain, but the following factors could account for the rise in cases: the recycling of rendered bovine material back to cattle feed; the persistence of the infectious agent on the ground; and the transfer of the infectious agent *in utero* to calves. The last route of infection has been established with scrapie in sheep and would be expected in cattle. At the time of writing, four years and five months after the offal ban in July 1988, the number of cases still presenting suggest that this ban has probably had little impact on the epidemiology of BSE. This is further evidence that the increase in BSE cases in recent years is not related to offal but is due to vertical transmission.

The Tyrell Report

Southwood recommended the establishment of a second committee to look at certain aspects of BSE. The chairman was Dr David Tyrell. Their report was presented for publication in June 1989, but for some inexplicable reason was not published until January 1990 (Tyrell 1990). This caused a delay of several months in the prohibition of certain infected tissues entering the food chain. Moreover, these tissues were never removed from items already available at retail outlets, and presumably some dried, canned, and frozen foods containing substantial amounts of beef offal are still being purchased and consumed.

The most disturbing paragraph in the Tyrell Report is as follows (Tyrell 1989):

Many extensive epidemiological studies around the world have contributed to the current consensus view that scrapie is not causally linked with Creutzfeldt–Jakob Disease (CJD). It is urgent that the same reassurance can be given about the lack of effect of BSE on human health. The best way of doing this is to monitor all UK cases of CJD over the next two decades.

This paragraph begins with an accurate statement. It is true that there is no evidence linking sheep scrapie with CJD (there is also no evidence linking BSE with scrapie). It is also true that it would be desirable for reassurance to be given that BSE will not infect humans. But surely this should only be considered after the reassuring evidence has been obtained. The Governments issuing of assurances illustrates its attitude to food safety: the prime intent is to reassure the public, i.e. to maintain the commercial status quo. Taking curative action is very much a secondary consideration, particularly if it is costly.

The last sentence of this paragraph of the Tyrell Report quite amazingly states that such reassurance is to be achieved by seeing how many more people die of CJD in the next 20 years. CJD may already account for about 1 per cent of deaths (Roberts 1990) and might have been acquired from eating beef many years ago (see above). Therefore, the experiment to see how many of us survive has started.

Recommendations for the elimination of BSE and related organisms

Rendering (processing) plants

There is a clear case for the total prohibition of the use of the bone meal fraction from the rendered remains of affected species. Rather, this product should be used as a fertilizer for cereal crops. This would interrupt the potentially dangerous cycle animal→ remains→ animal. Protein supplements for animal and poultry feeds should be obtained from fish or vegetable sources (e.g. soya).

It may be difficult to ensure that such a recommendation be enforced. One way might be to put all the rendering plants under direct Government control. There will also need to be legislation and surveillance procedures to ensure that imported products comply with these stipulations.

Replacement of BSE-infected herds with BSE-free stock

Since the frequency of vertical transmission of the infectious agent has not yet been defined and there is no way of identifying symptomless but infected animals, there is pressure to develop BSE-free herds now. BSE herds would presumably have to be kept in new pastures and thoroughly cleaned buildings. The following detailed proposals should eliminate BSE, but will be extremely costly to implement:

1. There should be a policy that no calves be reared from infected herds.
2. Any calf born in the near future from a cow belonging to an infected herd should be destroyed.
3. Milk-producing cows from infected herds should be slaughtered and incinerated at the end of their useful lactation. The carcass should not enter any part of the food chain.
4. Beef cattle should be slaughtered as soon as possible—preferably under 18 months of age. Careful removal of meat from the carcass might produce some relatively safe product for people over, say, 50. The brain, spinal cord, and body cavities containing 'high risk' material should not be manipulated. After removal of meat, the remainder of the carcass should be incinerated.
5. A system of introduction and documentation of BSE-free stock will be required. Every BSE-free animal should be required to be identified according to a pedigree indicating source and subsequent movements.
6. Urgent research must be done to quantify the extent to

which herds are infected but do not show signs of disease. Subsequently, any infected herds should be managed by the procedures outlined above.

DISCUSSION

To be fair, we must consider the counter-arguments over the two specific issues highlighted with intensive rearing—Salmonella in eggs and the epidemiology of BSE. The analysis by North and Gorman (1990) suggests that the risk of Salmonella in eggs has been greatly exaggerated for the following reasons.

1. *The instances when any individual has been proved to have suffered from Salmonella food poisoning are exceedingly rare*. This is not disputed, but surely the failure to identify the source of more cases of Salmonella food poisoning is because eggs are not labelled with the identity of the farm but only with that of the packing station. Most packing stations receive eggs from many farms.
2. *There are insufficient numbers of Salmonella in an egg to cause food poisoning*. This belief is based on experiments with healthy volunteer prison inmates in the USA who were fed varying amounts of *S. typhimurium*. The general conclusion of these experiments was that 10^6–10^8 salmonellae were needed to induce food poisoning. However, we cannot extrapolate these findings generally, certainly not to vulnerable people where lower numbers may be infectious. Moreover, Salmonella within egg yolk may be protected from the destructive effect of stomach acid because of the fatty nature of the yolk contents.
3. *Most Salmonella food poisoning is caused by lapses of hygiene*. There is no dispute that poor hygiene can cause food poisoning. However, the issue with Salmonella food poisoning is the extraordinary rise since 1985 in the numbers of just one species, i.e. *S. enteritidis*, and predominantly just

one type, i.e. type 4. The only common natural reservoir of this bacterium is poultry and the only food difficult to cook, or often eaten raw, is the egg. Of course some person-to-person spread of this bacterium may occur following ingestion of poultry products.

Many readers might hope that free-range eggs (in the real sense) might be safer than battery eggs. Unfortunately this is not so. The reason for the contamination of both types of eggs by Salmonella is the use of the same breeding flocks for free-range and battery production. This is not to decry free-range husbandry, because such methods must be expected to produce eggs superior in nutrients and taste relative to battery products, and surely no-one will dispute that free-range farming is associated with less cruelty.

Yet it is the cheap supermarket battery egg that is most popular with the consumer. The colour of the shell and the yolk (often heightened by orange dye in the chicken feed) seem more important than nutrients or the need for freedom from Salmonella. The ridiculousness of the UK consumer's obsession for brown shells is brought home to roost when it is appreciated that the average American demands eggs with snow-white shells.

The author finds it rather difficult to express fairness to the UK Government over its action on BSE. However, it must be pointed out that at the time of writing (December 1992) there is a remote possibility that the Government's expectations on the epidemiology of BSE will be met. It is not quite outside the bounds of mathematical chance that the large number of BSE cases currently being reported (in December 1992) will suddenly decline in 1993, with the disease becoming extinct by the end of the decade. This optimism has been well-aired by Government spokesmen during 1992, and the hope is based on the introduction of the offal ban on 18 July 1988. It is argued that, since most BSE cows are aged 4–5 years at death, the effects of the offal ban will not be evident until 1993 and the recent increase in BSE cases was entirely to be expected on account of recycling of contaminated bovine organs back to cows in 1987–8.

However, the dates are now straining the arithmetical credibility of this hope. Let us first assume that the offal ban in July 1988 was generally adopted. Most of the artificial feed containing the putative infectious agent would have been given to cows in the winter, not the spring or summer because of available grass or pastures. This means that little offal would have been fed between March and July 1988, and if the average age of acquisition of BSE is accepted as being 6 months (Wilesmith *et al.* 1988) then two effects should have been see by the late autumn of 1992:

1. The number of BSE cases should have dropped dramatically to about one-third of the previous year. This manifestly has not happened.
2. The average age of BSE cattle in 1992 should have increased compared with 1991 and previous years. Unfortunately, ministers now refuse to provide the relevant information following formal written parliamentary questions (Hinchliffe 1992).

BSE does appear to be the worst possible calamity to arise from the procedures used to provide an abundance of cheap meat. It is fortunate that the disease is rare elsewhere in the world, with only 17 cases notified in Switzerland, a few in France, and one in Denmark by December 1992. Yet many other countries use recycled animal offal as livestock feed. To some extent the size of the British problem may be due to misfortune, whereby a few highly infectious tissues were incorporated in cattle feed some years ago. This could have been as long ago as the 1970s, with the disease remaining largely subclinical or unnoticed for several years.

Other countries have taken positive action to protect their populations from the risk of BSE, with 26 imposing various restrictions on the import of British beef and cattle. Positive and effective action from the British government is still awaited.

REFERENCES

Agren, J., Muje, P., Hanninen, O., Herranen, J., and Penttila, I. (1987). Seasonal variations of lipid fatty acids of borela freshwater fish species. *Comparative Biochemistry and Physiology B*, **88**, 905–9.

British Medical Journal, **294**, 31–2 (1987).

Brown, P. and Gajdusek, D. G. (1991). Survival of scrapie virus after 3 years' interment. *Lancet*, **337**, 269–70.

Brown, P., Liberski, P. P., Wolff, A., and Gajdusek, D. L. (1990). Resistance of scrapie infectivity to steam autoclaving after formaldehyde fixation and limited survival after ashing at 360°: practical and theoretical implications. *Journal of Infectious Diseases*, **115**, 393–9.

Communicable Disease Reports (1982–1988). PHLS Communicable Disease Surveillance Centre, London.

Coyle, E. F., Ribeiro, C. D., Howard, A. J., Palmer, S. R., Jones, H. I., Ward, L., and Rowe, B. (1988). *Salmonella enteritidis* phage type 4 infection in association with hens' eggs. *Lancet*, **11**, 1295.

Crawford, M. A. (1968). Fatty-acid ratios in free-living and domestic animals. *Lancet*, **1**, 1329–32.

Crawford, M. and Marsh, D. (1989). *The driving force. Food evolution and the future*. Heinemann, London.

Dealler, S. F. and Lacey, R. W. (1990). Transmissible spongiform encephalopathies: the threat of BSE to man. *Food Microbiology*, **7**, 253–79.

Denton, M. and Lacey, R. W. (1991). Intensive farming and food processing: implications for polyunsaturated fats. *Journal of Nutritional Medicine*, **2**, 179–89.

Doreau, M., Batisse, V., and Bauchart, D. (1989). Appreciation de l'hydogenation des acides gras alimentaires dans le rumen de la vache: etude methodologique preliminaire. *Annales de Zootechnie*, **38**, 139–44.

Hinchliffe, D. (1992). PQ147, Priority Written 33. *Hansard*, October 29.

Hopper, S. A. and Mawer, S. (1988). *Salmonella enteritidis* in a commercial laying flock. *Veterinary Record*, **123**, 351.

Hulan, H. W., Ackman, R. G., Ratnayake, W. M. N., and Proudfoot, F. G. (1988). Omega-3 fatty acid levels and performance of broiler chickens fed red fish meal or red fish oil. *Canadian Journal of Animal Science*, **68**, 533–47.

Humphrey, T. J. (1992). Personal communication.

Humphrey, T. J., Mead, G. C., and Rowe, B. (1988) Poultry meat as a source of human salmonellosis in England and Wales. *Epidemiology and Infection*, **100**, 175–84.

Kromann, N. and Green, A. (1980). Epidemiological studies in the Upernavik district, Greenland. *Acta Medica Scandinaviea*, **208**, 401–6.

Lacey, R. W. (1991). *Unfit for human consumption*. Souvenir Press, London, 1–239.

Lancet (1988) *Salmonella enteritidis* phage type 4: chicken and egg. *Lancet*, **ii**, 720–2.

Lister, S. A. (1988). *Salmonella enteritidis* infection in broilers and broiler breeders. *Veterinary Record*, **123**, 350.

Miller, M. F., Shackleford, S. D., Hayden, K. D., and Reagan, J. O. (1990). Determination of the alteration in fatty acid profiles, sensory characteritics and carcass traits of swine fed elevated levels of monounsaturated fats in the diet. *Journal of Animal Science*, **68**, 1624–31.

North, R. and Gorman, T. (1990). *Chickengate*. Institute of Economic Affairs, London.

O'Brien, J. D. P. (1988). *Salmonella enteritidis* infection in boiler chickens. *Veterinary Record*, **122**, 214.

Perales, I. and Audicana, A. (1988). *Salmonella enteritidis* and eggs. *Lancet*, **ii**, 1133.

Prusiner, S. B. (1989). Scrapie prions. *Annual Review of Microbiology*, **43**, 345–74.

Rammel, C. G., Pearson, A. B., and Bentley, G. R. (1988). Vitamin E. selenium and polyunsaturated fatty acids in clinically normal grower (9–16 weeks pigs) and their feed: their relationship to the vitamin E/selenium deficiency ("VESD") syndrome. *New Zealand Veterinary Journal*, **36**, 133–7.

Rhee, K. S., Davidson, T. L., Knabe, D. A., Cross, H. R., Ziprin, Y. A., and Rhee, K. C. (1988). Effect of dietary high-oleic sunflower oil on pork carcass traits and fatty acid profiles of raw tissues. *Meat Science*, 24, 249–60.

Roberts, G. W. (1990). Memorandum submitted to the House of Commons Committee on Agriculture, 10 July 1990. HMSO, London.

Royal College of Physicians and British Cardiac Society (1976). Prevention of coronary heart disease. *Journal of the Royal College of Physicians*, **10**, 213–75.

Saunders, R. L. and Farrell, A. P. (1988). Coronary arteriosclerosis in Atlantic salmon. No regression of lesions after spawning. *Arteriosclerosis*, **8**, 378–84.

St. Louis, M. E., Dale, L. M., Potter, M. E., Thomas, M. D., Guzewich, J. J., Tauxe, R. V., and Blake, P. A. (1988). The emergence of grade A eggs as a major source of *Salmonella enteritidis* infections. *Journal of the American Medical Association*, **259**, 2103–7.

Simopoulos, A. P. and Salem, N. (1986). Purslane: a terrestial source of omega-3 fatty acids. *New England Journal of Medicine*, **315**, 833.

Simopoulos, A. P. and Salem, N. (1989). *n*-3 Fatty acids in eggs from range-fed Greek chickens. *New England Journal of Medicine*, **319**, 1412.

Southwood, R (1989). *Report of the Working Party on Bovine Spongiform Encephalopathy*. HMSO, London.

Tyrell, D. A. J. (1990). *Consultative Committee on Research into Spongiform Encephalopathies, Interim Report*. HMSO, London.

White, B. G., Ingalls, J. R., Sharma, H. R., and McKirdy, J. A. (1987). The effect of whole sunflower seeds on the flow of fat and fatty acids through the gastrointestinal tract of cannulated holstein steers. *Canadian Journal of Animal Science*, **67**, 447–59.

Wilesmith, J. W., Wells, G. A., Cranwell, M. P., and Ryan, J. B. (1988). Bovine spongiform encephalopathy: epidemiological studies. *Veterinary Record*, **123** (25) 638–44.

4

'Water is best': would Pindar still think so?

John Bowman

Dr John Bowman CBE is a freelance consultant and until June 1993 was Managing Director of Brown & Root Environmental. He graduated from the University of Reading and was awarded his doctorate at the University of Edinburgh. After a year as a postdoctoral Fellow at North Carolina State University, Dr Bowman returned to Reading in 1966 as Professor of Animal Production, a post which he held for fifteen years in addition to the parallel appointments of Head of the Department of Agriculture, Director of the University Farms, and Director of the Centre for Agricultural Strategy. In 1981 he left Reading University in order to take up the post of Secretary of the Natural Environment Research Council. In 1989 Dr Bowman was appointed Chief Executive of the National Rivers Authority. He is the author of several books on animal husbandry.

INTRODUCTION

'Water is best' is an inscription taken from the Roman baths at Aquae Sulis, or Bath as it is now known. The quote is attributed to Pindar, a poet born in Greece in 522 BC, and is taken from the first Olympian ode dedicated to the honour of Hieron of Syracuse. This poem was famed in antiquity for its brilliant use of metaphor, drawing on the beauty of nature to describe the athletic prowess of Greek heroes (Kirkwood 1982). The opening line 'water is best' expresses the widespread belief of the Greeks, and later the Romans, that water was the basic element and source of life. The Romans went to great lengths to ensure the purity of their water supplies. The aqueducts carrying water from clean springs far outside the Roman cities throughout their empire to individual houses, to streets for sewage disposal and to municipal bathing facilities testify to the importance placed on good water quality and management.

The aim of this discussion is to show that the Greeks and Romans were right to show a great reverence towards water, for life originated in water and it is water that makes life possible. Since water is readily available to most of us in the industrialized world, it is easy to take it for granted as a limitless gift of nature. Gift of nature it may be but limitless it is not, for although fresh water is a renewable resource, the total amount of water on the planet is finite. The physical, chemical, and biological systems of this planet have a great capacity to cleanse fresh water; unfortunately, man's capacity for pollution is accelerating fast with the growth in population and in agricultural and industrial development across the globe. Locally available water resources may very quickly be exhausted through over-abstraction or become useless due to pollution. It is ironic that, through greed and ignorance, water can become a bringer of death and disease rather than life.

In the time of Pindar, the world was a much cleaner place with humans having only a local effect on water resources rather than the global effect they have now. In this chapter I plan to show how human activities change water quality and endanger the lives of us all even if we live in countries which do make determined efforts to treat and conserve water wisely. In Britain, one of the first countries to experience urbanization and subsequently industrialization, the problems of deteriorating water quality were realized and, in this century, a subsequent improvement was achieved once we had seen the error of our early ways. Fortunately for us that process took 300 years—a period long enough for mistakes to be made and solutions to be found at a rate comparable with our development. Today, many countries around the world are being transformed by the same processes of rapid population growth, urbanization, and industrialization but over a period spanning a few decades at most. Such countries are trying to improve their standard of living by adopting technology and processes from the developed world whilst not appreciating that the technology may be inappropriate and that they may not have sufficient management skills to make the processes work effectively. One important consequence is that the need to avoid pollution and to safeguard water resources and quality does not have the priority it should have. Whilst in many cases the adverse effects are generally local there is increasing evidence that some pollution is widespread and, especially by atmospheric transfer and water migration, is leading to global damage.

Water-borne diseases and diseases transmitted by vectors which live in the water environment account for about a third of all deaths in the world. The major proportion of these water-related deaths are in developing and tropical countries and most of them can be attributed to inadequate supplies of water for drinking, for personal hygiene, and for sewage disposal. It is not only water quantity which is the culprit. The quality of water and the management practices associated with agricultural water, water for industry, and the management of natural areas of water, the home of water disease vectors, can all be blamed for causing a large proportion of human deaths. The problems are extensive whilst the technical solutions are generally known and available. It is money, education, and motivation which are in short supply.

Global problems have to be addressed by all the nations of the world working in concert. Those countries fortunate enough to have the experience, the skills, and the financial resources to contribute must do so. The solutions to the world's environmental problems must be based on the principal objective of sustainable development. Fresh water, a finite but renewable resource must be used so that we leave our descendants with at least the same opportunities to develop their lives which we inherited. I am sure Pindar would have had the same opinion.

GLOBAL WATER RESOURCES

Sources of fresh water

There is a considerable quantity of water on the Earth but most of it is in an unsuitable form for man's requirements. It is estimated that there are 4×10^9 km^3 of water on the planet of which 97 per cent is saline and not generally useful without treatment. The remaining 3 per cent is fresh water and is found in rivers, lakes, underground aquifers, and locked up as ice. In fact, 79 per cent of fresh water is in the form of ice, mainly in the two polar ice sheets and in the high mountain glaciers. Little of the polar ice is used by humans but the mountain ice and snow fields are an important source of melt-water supply in countries adjoining the Alps, the Himalayas, the Andes, and other mountain regions. Twenty per cent of fresh water is in underground aquifers where the retention time may vary from a few years in some places to thousands of years in others. A good example of the latter is found under the deserts of what is now Libya, Egypt, Chad, and the Sudan. Such water is termed palaeolithic, is in very large underground lakes, but is essentially non-renewable. Yet it is being tapped for municipal and agricultural supplies for the coastal regions of Libya involving the largest well and pipeline scheme in the world. A mere 1 per cent of the world's fresh water is found in rivers and lakes. Retention time in surface waters is also very variable. For short, fast-flowing rivers in Britain the time from precipitation on the catchment at the river's source to reaching the sea may be a matter of days. By contrast, for a large river like the Ganges the time from source to sea will be weeks, and the flow time is substantially affected by the nature of the soil type and vegetation cover.

Fortunately for humans, the physical properties of water, combined with solar energy, provide a means of renewing and redistributing fresh water around the planet. This process of evaporation and precipitation is known as the hydrological cycle. Every year the thermal energy of the sun evaporates about 454×10^3 km^3 fresh water from the oceans and seas. In addition, a further 72×10^3 km^3 is evaporated from the land and from transpiration by plants. Of the water evaporated about 110×10^3 km^3 falls back on the land as precipitation. This leaves a difference of 38×10^3 km^3 between the water that leaves the land and the fresh water that falls back onto it. This excess over precipitation is the basic quantity of renewable fresh water found as surface water, ground water, and run-off (Milaradov 1990).

Until 200 years ago, human populations had developed at a pace which allowed agricultural and domestic water needs to be met from locally available sources. When water resources failed in times of drought or when population outstripped supply, communities failed or were forced to migrate to new sites. There is ample evidence of this sort of population movement happening thousands of years ago in the Middle East. Similar movements have taken place in the Sahel in the last 20 years.

Today, three factors are changing the ability of populations in Third World countries to meet their water needs. These are the rapid increase in population numbers, the urbanization of the population, and their increasing dependence on industry as compared with agriculture as a source of earning a living. As a consequence there is a growing disparity between per capita water supply and demand in these countries. In the semi-arid and arid regions of the world socio-economic development is encountering a 'water barrier'. The requirements for water in these circumstances are leading to the development of very substantial civil engineering projects such as dams, reservoirs, and long-distance, large-diameter water pipelines. Such developments do not necessarily ensure a water supply indefinitely and there may inevitably be a fall in water supply and quality for millions of people associated with a falling standard of living and a greater risk to health.

The population increase has to be fed. This means an increase in the scale and intensity of agriculture coupled with an increase in the demand for water for irrigation. In some countries water scarcity is already apparent even where some substantial dams and water transfer schemes have been built. For example, in Egypt water for irrigation is inadequate even though two dams have been built on the Nile this century (Ghali 1992). Further water storage schemes are contemplated, with severe consequences for other adjacent countries dependent for water on the Nile. Such conflicts over scarce resources are likely to become more common and are likely to lead to political difficulties.

The urban population of the Third World is estimated to have grown from 300 million to 1200 million over the past 20 years. A continuation of this trend would lead to almost half the world's population living in urban areas by the end of the century. However, it is not just the increase in population in urban areas which represents the whole of the supply problem. The legitimate aspirations of those populations for an improving standard of living will also lead to a subsantial additional requirement for water of high quality to the new cities. Third World countries are keen to develop their industrial economies. Water for industry will therefore be an increasing need.

Current estimates show that world water need is set to grow as a whole, although demand in the developed nations is static and may even drop with the increased use of recycling techniques. Figure 4.1 shows the trends in water demand by continent. If the people of the developing nations are to enjoy satisfactory water quality, management and treatment techniques must grow in line with population, as well as agricultural and industrial development.

USES OF FRESH WATER

The principal uses of water can be defined under five major categories. These are as follows.

1. Municipal: public water supply for drinking, personal hygiene, sewage disposal, and drainage.
2. Agriculture and fisheries: the main use is for irrigation but there are also quantities needed for livestock and for fish farming.

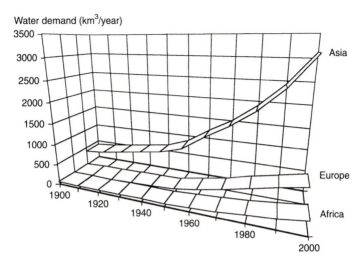

Fig. 4.1. Global trends in water demand. Source: UNEP/WHO 1988.

3. Industry: substantial amounts are used in a variety of industrial processes such as paper-making and as cooling water in power stations.
4. Recreation: water contact sports (sailing and swimming) and fishing.
5. Environment: aesthetic enjoyment of water-dependent landscapes and wildlife.

Each of these uses gives rise to substantial water quantity requirements but also to important differences in the quality of the water that should be available. The quality is important for the effective achievement of the activity concerned and also for the minimization of risk to human health. In some cases it is quite possible, and sometimes essential if supply requirements are to be met, to use the same water for more than one purpose, although this adds to the care and treatment needed in the provision of supply. Figure 4.2 shows the predicted trends in

Water use (km³/year)

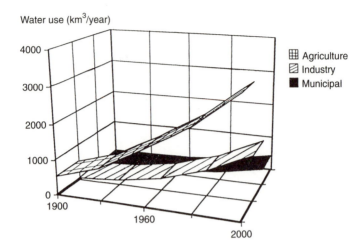

Fig. 4.2. Trends in global water use. Source: UNEP/WHO 1988.

water use up to the end of the century. Globally, irrigation and the production of food account for two-thirds of human requirements.

As the human population increases from the present level exceeding 5 billion to 8 or 10 billion in the middle of the next century there will be a need to expand the amount of irrigated farmland by a similar proportion. In turn, this will require an increase in water for irrigation. Even in 1988 UNEP/WHO anticipated that by the year 2000 the water required for irrigation will be equivalent to the total world water use in 1980. An adverse effect of the increase in irrigation will be an accompanying increase in the land subject to problems of salinization and waterlogging. These problems already affect about 10 per cent of the 270 million hectares of intensively irrigated land. Salinization is increasing at such a rate that irrigated land is going out of production at up to 50 per cent of the rate at which new land is being brought into production. The amount of new land which can be effectively brought into production is very limited in the absence of irrigation water thus requiring more intensive use of current agricultural land. Also, it is worth noting that there is ample opportunity to increase the effectiveness with which current irrigation water is used. Between 50 and 80 per cent of irrigation water is lost through early evaporation, leakage, inappropriate techniques, and bad management (UNEP/WHO 1988).

The increasing human population will also lead to the need for increased water supply and sewage disposal facilities. Good management and the application of appropriate treatment technology has already shown that potentially hazardous water sources and waste water can be turned into supplies suitable for re-use by humans, for domestic supply, for agriculture, or for industry. Water in the River Thames in the United Kingdom is estimated to be used for potable supply eleven times in its journey down stream before it eventually reaches the sea. In the arid nations of the Middle East the use of industrial and municipal waste-water may go some way to meeting agricultural needs. Figure 4.3 shows the water demands in Jordan for

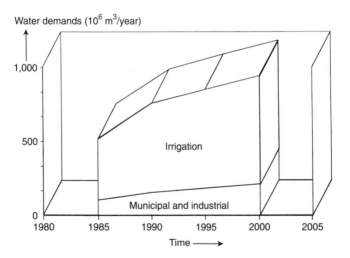

Fig. 4.3. Water demands in Jordan. Source: Arar 1987.

municipal/industrial and irrigation uses respectively. It can be seen that municipal and industrial water could meet 30 per cent of irrigation demand. To achieve high levels of re-use will probably require intervention by government through education, financial incentives, and regulation. Exhortation alone will not be adequate.

Most water uses lead to a change in water quality. In most cases the changes are for the worse. This is because a lot of municipal and industrial water is used to carry away effluents such as sewage and by-product chemicals and heat. In agriculture, the water is carrying away plant nutrients, herbicides, insecticides, and animal faeces. Much can be done by careful activity management to reduce the amount of waste to be discharged. Much can also be done to prevent water deterioration by the application of on-site effluent control and treatment. The practice of using water to dilute and disperse unwanted chemicals and organic matter as well as potential human and animal disease organisms has to be carefully monitored and used as infrequently as possible.

Municipal water

Only about 1 per cent of the fresh water used is for municipal supply purposes and of this only a small proportion is used for drinking. Almost any source of water, including sea water, can be used for municipal supply purposes. However, it is perhaps obvious that the cleaner and less contaminated the basic source the less treatment will be needed. The extent of treatment required affects the cost of supply provision. Also, the final quality is affected in many ways by the treatment process and may be considered unsuitable or even unacceptable for reasons of poor taste and colour or other adverse traits such as degree of hardness. It is most desirable to find basic sources which require minimal treatment to provide drinking water in compliance with World Health Organization (WHO) guidelines.

In spite of the extent of urbanization and industrialization over several centuries in developed countries the basic sources of supply are still generally of good quality and require minimal treatment. There is increasing concern that some ground water sources have been affected by industrial spillages and poor waste disposal practices. There is also mounting concern that the same sources are being contaminated by agrochemicals perhaps overgenerously applied over the last few decades. Both these concerns have led to increased treatment costs and to greater efforts to safeguard ground waters by restricting the activities on the surface from which the water recharges the ground water. In the developing countries, the combination of population growth, urbanization, and industrialization together with a lack of effective treatment facilities is causing communities to use inferior sources and to accept inferior supplies.

Sewage disposal and treatment is in most developed countries adequate to safeguard the sources of water supply. The water from such sources may also be of a sufficient standard to allow its re-use for municipal supply. However, in marked contrast, the same does not generally apply in developing countries. Inadequate control of sewage disposal leads to contaminated sources which may require more treatment for supply than is locally available or can be afforded. There are many examples of rivers in the developing world which are heavily contaminated by sewage effluent and other waste discharges as they pass through major cities. The rivers in these cases are used as open waste disposal channels even though they may also be the main local source of municipal water supplies. Treatment costs to produce good quality drinking water from a river with high levels of contamination will be much higher than for cleaner rivers in developed nations which are subject to stringent discharge controls.

It is not sufficiently recognized that only a small proportion of the water used from municipal supplies is used for drinking. A much larger amount is used for sewage and waste disposal. Yet the standards which apply to the quality of municipal supply are those needed for the water to be fit to drink. Separate supplies for drinking and for other municipal uses would allow some reduction in treatment costs but would obviously increase distribution costs. In most of the world a two-supply system has not been adopted although it might be considered that this is the case where bottled water is provided for drinking and piped water for other purposes.

The quality of drinking water must be considered the most important single issue regarding water quality at present. Of the 5000 million people on the planet, one-third do not have safe drinking water. The death toll due to water-borne disease alone is 50 000 per day or one-third of all deaths occurring in the world (Bays 1992). Thus, the most important requirements related to human water consumption are those of microbiological content and hygienic acceptability. It is the poor quality of water with respect to these factors that cause the majority of water-related illnesses in the developing world.

Of lesser importance but still very significant for human health are the organic and inorganic compounds. At some generally lower concentration these substances may be essential for health but above certain levels they may be injurious. Excessive concentrations of nitrates and fluorides are known to cause blood disorders and skeletal problems respectively. Metal ions such as cadmium and aluminium can damage the nervous system and upset the human metabolism. Organic compounds such as benzene and many pesticides are known carcinogens, and as such cause increased risk of tumour formation. Excessive concentrations of particulates and salinity can cause illness, but since they can be tolerated at much greater concentrations than most other substances they really pose aesthetic rather than health problems.

Agriculture and fisheries

Globally, agriculture accounts for about three-quarters of all fresh water used by man. Most of this is for irrigation. Since, as indicated earlier, there are enormous losses of water from the irrigation systems adopted there is plenty of opportunity to irrigate more crops using the same volume of water.

Generally, the production of crops is not affected by the use of polluted irrigation water where the pollution is organic compounds and microbiological and biological organisms. However, there is considerable risk of debilitating disease and death for those farmers and their families who have to tend their crops where they are working with and in contaminated irrigation water. Sewage and waste-water have been used for thousands of years as crop fertilizers but with increasing intensity of agriculture and increasing density of the human population there is a need to be more strict in the way in which sewage and wastes are used as an agricultural resource. Irrigated water which is polluted with organic and inorganic compounds arising from agricultural pesticides or from industrial wastes can affect the growth and yield of crops. Furthermore, crops grown in these circumstances may accumulate quantities of the organic and inorganic compounds. Though the crop yield may not be affected and in some cases may be enhanced, there may be considerable risk of illness amongst the consumers.

Fresh-water fisheries are an important source of food in many parts of the world as well as providing one of the most important recreation activities. In the developed world, the pressure from anglers helps to keep the general public aware of water pollution and environmental issues. Like plants, it is well-established that fish living in water containing organic and inorganic pollutants will concentrate these substances in their tissues. In many cases the substances are not concentrated evenly throughout the fish but selectively in particular body organs or tissues. Clearly, people who eat such fish may be, and have been, subject to poisoning and death. Thirty years ago, there was particular concern over the levels of heavy metals in many rivers in the developed world. As a result there was sufficient public pressure and political will to introduce more stringent discharge controls and to remove some of the sources of pollution. This is not now seen as a major general concern but there are still some local situations where heavy metal pollution needs to be watched and action taken. Estuaries and ports are examples where the silt which accumulates may contain high levels of heavy metals from industrial discharges. If left undisturbed the silt represents no hazard, but as soon as the silt is disturbed then the heavy metals may find their way into the food chain via fish. The pollution levels may still represent a hazard to fish and man in rivers in Eastern Europe where pollution controls have been ignored. The poor water quality in rivers such as the Volga and the Danube is indicative of what can happen in the absence of rigorous control of industrial wastes.

Perhaps the best known and most worrying example of heavy metal poisoning in humans via fish was the mercury poisoning of fishermen in Minimata Bay in Japan in the 1960s (Chapman 1992). However, this case can be seen by hindsight to be an exception, albeit a tragic one, which emphasized to the world the precautions necessary to safeguard fishermen and their customers.

Industry

Globally, about 20 per cent of the fresh water used is for industry. In the developed world it is likely that industry will tend to use less water in future. However, in developing countries, as their economies expand, water requirements for industry may increase unless they adopt rapidly the water saving technology of the developed world.

Industry of many kinds has the potential to cause serious pollution of surface and ground waters. The chemical wastes from a wide range of industries can leak or be carelessly discharged into water-courses and thence into treatment supply networks. During this century higher standards of water use and waste management, together with more stringent controls by regulation on the discharges which industry may make, has reduced substantially the risks of this source of pollution. However, there is still much to be done and the practice of using rivers and lakes as a convenient means of disposing of industrial wastes throughout the world needs to be severely curtailed.

As a consequence of the increase in industrial discharge controls and in the costs of water supply and treatment, industry is reducing wherever possible the use of water and the amount of waste discharged. Industrial systems using complete recycling of water and zero discharge are now in operation and are likely to become increasingly common. By this means it is possible to see the adverse impact of industry on water-quality declining substantially in future.

Recreation

The need for water for recreational activities is on the increase but still of much lesser importance than the other uses detailed above. In developed countries, swimming and water contact sports such as sailing and canoeing are increasing. Links have been established between contaminated water contact and the occurrence of illness such as gastrointestinal infections, but the incidence of serious disease is very small. Similar small risks may arise from contact with water which is nutrient rich and polluted, in which organisms such as 'blue-green algae' thrive and produce highly deleterious toxins. Incidents of this type are few but increasing.

Environment

Water is obviously essential to the maintenance of all biological resources and to the continuation of most aesthetically desirable landscapes. It is therefore important to general social well-being. A particular aspect of such well-being relates to tourism, especially in developing countries where such activity may represent an important part of foreign currency earnings. Tourists are not willing to visit sites where the water is dirty and unhygienic and they therefore represent a welcome incentive to improve water quality and the environment as a whole. The effect of reduced tourism on local economies and development schemes should not be underestimated.

WATER QUALITY

In order to understand how fresh water has altered since the time of Pindar it is necessary to refer to some modern concepts of water quality measurement. Water quality is generally described through a set of variables relating to the physico-chemical and biological properties of the water. These variables have been used over many years, and are constantly being modified and expanded as analytical techniques develop and as the range of substances produced by the chemical industry increases. The problem of setting standards for water quality becomes even more complex as the ability to measure substances in ever more minute concentrations becomes possible.

The importance of substances in a water source is dependent on the purpose for which it is to be used. For this reason, various groups of water users have developed their own methods for describing water quality. Only the water quality issues that affect human health or standard of living will be considered here. Apart from the health effects of water quality, it is important to consider both the aesthetic beauty of water in the landscape and, since some recreational pursuits depend on water, its contribution to our standard of living. With this in mind water quality variables can be grouped into the following categories:

- microbiological organisms
- particulate matter
- salinity
- organic pollutants
- inorganic pollutants.

A short description of each of these categories now follows.

Microbiological and biological organisms

Many organisms are found in fresh water which have an effect on human health. These include species of viruses, bacteria, protozoa, and algae for which the whole life-cycle of the organism is found in the fresh water. Other species such as parasitic worms and insects have only some stages of their life-cycle in fresh water, whilst other stages occur in the hosts which they parasitize or in the other media such as air and soil. Some of the organisms do not themselves affect human health but are hosts to disease organisms. They act as disease vectors by transferring the disease organism from an affected human or animal to other humans and animals. The extent of their occurrence depends not only on the extent of the natural environment where they can thrive but also on the behaviour of man and the way in which he manages his livestock and the natural environment, including fresh water. Thus, humans and animals which are hosts to the organisms will usually excrete the organisms in their faeces and urine. The existence of high levels of the organisms in fresh water is related to the extent to which human and animal excreta from contaminated individuals are returned to fresh water. This can happen through direct defecation into waterways and by faeces deposited on land being washed off by rain and snow. The isolation of infected individuals and livestock, the clear transfer and separation of faeces and urine to treatment works, and the careful disposal of sewage solids and separated treated water are the measures needed to ensure that disease organisms do not thrive.

Particulates

Particulates in fresh water are of two sorts, inorganic and organic. The former are generally silicate or other rock particles which have been washed into river or lake by precipitation and run-off or have originated from scouring of the river bed. Inorganic particles may also include metal compounds from ore-bearing rocks or from waste streams from industry. In low concentrations these may not represent a problem to the water user or be a health hazard. However, in some areas where the rocks contain high levels of mineral ores and where industrial pollution is severe health risks will be substantial. Special treatment measures will be needed to make the water suitable for municipal, agricultural, or industrial purposes. There is also the problem of disposing of the material taken from the water during treatment if further pollution is to be avoided.

Organic particles which represent natural decaying plant material or human or animal faeces may also have reached fresh water from run-off or from waste discharges. The particular importance of the organic content of water is that it affects the oxygen availability. Many of the organisms responsible for breaking down organic matter require oxygen for metabolism. The higher the organic content the higher the oxygen demand. Oxygen depletion can often become so severe that fish and other species are killed and the whole microbial balance of the water body is disturbed. The oxygen content is a key indicator of water quality and the load of organic material in the water.

The chemistry of organic particles in fresh water is complex and includes metal ion binding properties which may cause health risks and make the water unsuitable for other uses. Problems of colour, taste, and smell may be associated with the organic content of water which, whilst offensive if the water is used for municipal supply, may not be a health hazard. It is important, however, to control the amount of faecal organic matter getting into fresh water bodies if the normal water environment is to be maintained.

One of the main causes of substantial silting in rivers in recent years has been the extent of new deforestation in developing countries. This leads to much more rapid run-off of precipitation, to shorter retention time for water in the soil, and to greater extremes of flood and drought conditions. The additional particles in the water supply, whilst reducing its quality, are not the major disbenefit. It is an excess or conversely a shortage of water which has the main effect on human health.

Salinity

Salinity, largely caused by sodium salts, is an important characteristic in determining the quality of water. For most uses fresh water containing low levels of salt is essential. High levels are undesirable and salt intrusion into fresh-water sources is to be avoided. The content of salts in fresh waters is the result of several factors, including the salt content of the soils and rocks over or underlaying the water body. The main sources of saline intrusion are irrigation waters and over-abstraction of ground waters in coastal areas and islands adjoining large salt-water bodies. Two examples of contemporary problems will illustrate the point. In eastern England, which is gradually sinking relative to sea-level, abstraction of fresh water from underground sources is causing salt water from the North Sea to move westwards and to contaminate the ground water. Similarly, in the coastal region of Libya, steady and heavy abstraction of underground waters is allowing the Mediterannean to move south and penetrate the ground waters. In each case, the rate of abstraction has exceeded the natural rate of ground-water recharge, thus stimulating the saline intrusion. Other sources of saline contamination include salt-spreading on roads to prevent ice and snow problems and waters from mines and oil wells.

The main cause of salinity problems is poor irrigation practice. Waterlogging followed by evaporation will deposit salt in the soil and the constant flow of irrigation water will strip salt from the soil and deposit it when the water evaporates. Much is now known as to how these problems can be avoided by alternative irrigation systems, but the damage done in the past is considerable.

In humans, ingestion of salt water causes vomiting, and continued ingestion will cause hypertension and eventual madness. Some plant species are salt tolerant but the important agricultural crops are not. Where agricultural land becomes saline, food production is reduced or ceases. For industry, salt water may be used for some applications but it usually gives rise to process engineering problems albeit with no direct effects on human health.

Acidity

There is much natural variation in the acidity of fresh waters. This arises from the variation in the substances in the soils and rocks around and through which the water passes and which go into solution in the water. The degree of acidity will determine the substances which dissolve into the water from the surrounding rocks. Rain and snow are naturally slightly acid due to the presence of dissolved carbon dioxide from the atmosphere. The natural fauna and flora in acid and alkaline waters are usually different but adapted to the conditions.

Over the past 300 years, man has added increasing quantities of sulphur dioxide to the atmosphere from coal burning in power stations, in factories, and in houses. Also, over the past 100 years, increasing quantities of nitrogen oxides have been emitted from internal combustion engines. These sulphur and nitrogen gases have been precipitated in the form of weak acids in rain and snow. This acid precipitation may be local but because gases are carried long distances in the atmosphere it may also descend hundreds of miles from the source of the gas emissions. Much of the acid rain over the United Kingdom originates from gases emitted in Germany whilst much of the gases emitted in the United Kingdom, for instance, is precipitated as acid rain over Scandinavia, depending on the prevailing wind direction.

The health risk to humans from more acidic waters arises not directly from the acid but from the metals which the acid dissolves from the rocks surrounding fresh water. Enhanced levels of heavy metals and especially aluminium in fresh water which arise in this way are deleterious to plants, particularly trees, and also to fish. In the more extreme cases lakes and rivers may become devoid of life. At high concentrations metals dissolved in drinking water can be injurious to humans.

Measures to reduce the amount of acid rain are being actively pursued. These include using low sulphur coal, the fitting of gas desulphurization equipment to coal-fired power stations and other coal-fired processes. Such equipment is very expensive and gives rise to other deleterious environmental effects. Therefore, the need to reduce acid rain is a major contributory factor in some countries' moving from coal-fired power stations to other forms of electricity generation. To reduce nitrogen oxide emissions from internal combustion engines some countries require catalytic convertors to be fitted to all vehicles. This, too, is expensive.

Organic substances

As previously mentioned, the two main types of organic compounds in fresh water are plant biodegradation products and sewage degradation products. Both types cause a substantial demand for oxygen in the water by the bacteria and other organisms which continue the degradation of organic compounds to the eventual breakdown substances, carbon dioxide and water. Very large amounts of organic substances will cause oxygen to be totally depleted from the water by the micro-organisms.

Another minor, but nevertheless important, source of organic substances in fresh water is the class of substances known as the chlorinated micro-organics, widely used in industry and equally widely discharged into water. These substances can cause health problems in humans including mutations, cancer, and birth abnormalities. The main means of preventing these difficulties is to maintain stringent controls on discharges from industry and from sewage treatment plants.

Inorganic substances

There are many inorganic substances found in fresh water. They include some elements which are essential to human health. For example, iodine, fluorine, and selenium are provided almost entirely from drinking water. At the same time it has to be recognized that excess amounts of these elements can be injurious to health. Thus, high levels of iodine in drinking water can lead to problems in the human thyroid gland. A second group of substances in fresh water, which include iron and nitrates, can be tolerated up to a threshold level when drunk by humans. Above that level health can be impaired. Yet a third group of substances, which are mutagens and carcinogens, are deleterious to health at any content level. Most of these substances are pollutants, such as agrochemicals used for pest and plant disease control and industrial chemicals, which should not be allowed to get into water supplies at all.

The most ubiquitous inorganic substances in fresh-water are

the agricultural fertilizers which leach from farmland in substantial quantities. These are nitrates, ammonium salts, phosphates, and to a lesser extent potassium salts. High levels of nitrates and phosphates will lead to substantial growth of algae and to deoxygenation. In some cases, species of blue-green algae multiply and produce toxins which can directly cause injury to those who ingest or come into contact with them. In addition to chemical fertilizers, high nitrate levels can occur in surface and ground waters from the decomposition of plant material such as happens after ploughing up mature pasture.

This very brief summary of the main criteria used to categorize the quality of water emphasizes the complexity of the subject. It also emphasizes the need for careful and well-planned monitoring, for good sampling and analytical techniques, and for well-trained and intelligent management of water supply managers.

WATER-RELATED DISEASES

Water-related diseases and health problems can be considered in three groups; those where the disease organism (bacteria, virus, protozoa) lives in water at some stage in its life-cycle and causes disease in humans as a result of ingestion: those where the pathogen is transferred to humans by an animal vector such as an insect which lives in water: and those caused by ingestion of, or contact with, chemical pollutants and biologically produced toxins.

In terms of the obvious effects on human health and morbidity the first two groups are by far the most important. However, the third group, which is much more insidious, may account for a great deal of undetected deterioration in human capability. As a result of poor controls on industrial and agricultural effluents it may become much more important than the pathogenic disease problems in future.

So what sort of incidence of water-related diseases occur in the world and how many people die from these diseases? This is not an easy question to answer since the available statistics are not comprehensive. However, some indication of the magnitude of the health problem can be gauged from a few examples. Diarrhoea, caused by a large number of bacteria and viruses, probably accounts for over 5000 million infections and for over 10 million deaths per year, whilst amoebic dysentry affects over 400 million and accounts for a further 30 000 deaths per year (UNEP/WHO 1988). Cholera, which gains much attention, accounts for 50 000 deaths a year mainly in Africa and Asia (UNEP 1989).

Diseases which are transferred to humans by animal vectors have an even higher incidence and cause more deaths. Three examples will suffice. Four species of snail transmit the parasitic disease known as bilharzia or schistosomiasis, and all are prevalent in many developing nations (Feachem *et al.* 1983). The snails carry a worm which, for part of its lifecycle, lives in water. People who work or play in worm-infested water may be invaded by the worms through the skin. The worms once inside the human body cause organ damage. Worm eggs are excreted in faeces and urine whence they develop in the snails feeding on the faeces. Over 200 million people a year are infected and between 500 thousand and 1 million die each year from the infection (UNEP/WHO 1988). Malaria, transmitted by mosquitoes and caused by a trypanosome, is estimated to affect over 800 million people (UNEP/WHO 1988) and to cause 6 million deaths per year (UNEP 1989). Deaths have been as high as nearly 16 million in 1980 (UNEP 1989). The third example concerns onchocerciasis or river blindness which is transmitted by flies and caused by a worm. It was estimated that in 1983 nearly 18 million people were infected, of which over 300 thousand were blind, and that between 20 000 and 50 000 deaths occurred per year (UNEP/WHO 1988; UNEP 1989). For the third group of water-related health problems, caused by chemical ingestion and contact, there are no reliable figures of effect. Compared with the numbers recounted above they are infinitesimal.

Whilst the magnitude of the levels of infection and deaths itself indicates that much harm is done by these diseases, it is probably small compared to the sub-lethal harm which is caused. The debilitating effect on human performance is enormous and the loss of quality of life can only be guessed. The resources required to cope with curing the sick and to reduce the incidence of disease are a major call on the assets of countries struggling to survive at all. Countries with lesser problems and more resources must provide more help.

A HISTORY OF WATER SUPPLY AND QUALITY

This section gives a brief history of water supply and quality issues in Britain almost from the time of Pindar to the present day. Most of the water problems associated with a country changing from one with a low population density subsisting on agriculture in a rural economy, to one of high population density relying on industry and trade as well as agriculture with a mainly urban economy, have been experienced in Britain. Whilst by no means all Britain's water problems have been solved, they have been to the extent that there is a reliable supply of water suitable for municipal, agricultural, and industrial purposes. There is also a waste and sewage disposal system that does not cause widespread problems even though it could be sustantially improved. The population is not generally exposed to water health hazards. A study of the British experience would be useful to developing nations in determining their own water supply systems.

Roman Britain

Before AD 43 the population in Britain was probably a few hundred thousand, widely scattered throughout the country and living a largely pastoral way of life. The supply of clean water came from ponds and streams and with little pollution problem from sewage and waste disposal. The arrival of the Romans in that year caused some major changes as they brought with them a very different form of society which had proved successful in other parts of their empire. Roman civilization was based on a system of fortifications and administrative centres with much higher population densities. The towns which the Romans built required considerable engineering for water supply, especially in view of the Roman regard for water quality and personal hygiene (Davey 1964).

Even today it is possible to see in various parts of the former empire some of the sophisticated and extensive water supply and control methods used. The towns housed tens of thousands of people. For instance, it is estimated that Ephesus in modern Turkey had a population of about 125 000 in Roman times. In Rome, the capital and largest city in the Empire, water was brought to the city on nine aqueducts from natural springs in the surrounding area (Frontinus 1873). The water supply system included settling tanks and a pipe system to the larger homes. Public fountains were provided for the less affluent. There were water-flushing arrangements to keep homes and streets clean. Sewage was drained from public and private toilets. There were strict laws and penalties applying to water supplies which deterred the illegal taking of water and pollution. In these ways the Romans were able to develop quite large urban areas without encountering high levels of water-related disease. The Romans brought these techniques with them and developed them in building their British towns. The remains can be seen today in places like Bath, York, and Lincoln. The water distribution systems were both advanced and a serious health hazard. Water was piped using jointed pottery and lead pipes. This prevented pollution getting into the supplies and ensured a reliable supply of running water for sewage and waste disposal. However, lead was used not only for pipes but for table-ware, cutlery, and water storage cisterns as well. In areas of hard water such practice does not endanger health because lead is not soluble in such water. By contrast in areas of soft water, in which lead is soluble, the lead was ingested in the drinking water. The richer persons were most affected since they were the ones who could afford the lead piping. The collapse of the Roman Empire has been attributed by some to lead poisoning, which can cause infertility, dementia, and mental instability. The risks of drinking lead in water seem to have been known to the Romans but they are not thought to have taken steps to prevent it. In the first century AD Vitruvius stated that (Nriagu 1983)

'Water is much more wholesome when taken from earthenware pipes than from lead pipes. For it seems to be made injurious by lead, because white lead is produced from it; and this is harmful to the human body. Thus if what is produced by anything is injurious, it is not doubtful that the thing is not wholesome in itself.'

The Romans left Britain one relatively serious pollution problem. They developed mining for metal ores and the mine wastes deposited in upland streams fed metal compounds into the water supplies. In some upland areas even today the same problem exists. However, on balance there is no doubt that the Roman water systems were very effective in enabling people to live in densely populated towns whilst avoiding a lot of water-related disease.

The Middle Ages

When the Romans finally left Britain in AD 410 the population increased steadily as a result of Saxon migration from mainland Europe. In AD 1000 the population is put at between 1 and 2 million and this is thought to have grown to some 4 to 5 million by the year 1600, less than a tenth of today's population. The Saxons were a farming people who lived in relatively scattered settlements and pursued a very different lifestyle from the urban Romans. They did not maintain the Roman towns with their water supply systems and much of the infrastructure was lost. Because of the rural lifestyle this did not affect the Saxons' water supply which they could still obtain in good quality from wells and streams unpolluted by human waste (Longworth 1988).

Towns regained their importance for administration and trade from 1200 onwards. London, the largest city, at that time adjoining the river Thames which flowed over a much broader flood plain than today, experienced the classical water problems associated with urban development and similar to those seen in the developing world now. The first water supply in London was provided in 1237. This was piped from springs on a private estate to public fountains for public collection; a system similar to that which the Romans had developed 1500 years earlier in their empire. In London there is little evidence that private water supplies were provided before 1600. Then the New River was built to carry fresh water from a spring from Chadwell, Hertfordshire, to the city. For the best part of the next 200 years the citizens of London relied on buying water from professional water carries who obtained it from public water conduits. Meanwhile, the Thames became progressively more polluted, since the city had poor sanitation arrangements and much of the domestic sewage and waste was washed into the Thames and its tributaries. Over this period the population in Britain had grown to between 6 and 7 million by 1700, and a century later to 10 million. Apart from London and a few other urban centres the general population was able to get clean adequate water from streams nearby and the level of pollution, except in the towns, was not serious.

The effects of the Industrial Revolution

Along with the Industrial Revolution in the eighteenth century came the mass movement of people from the rural areas to the new towns to provide the labour for the new industries. The water supply systems were not developed to cope with the increasing urban population and people in the towns resorted to trying to obtain their supplies from local streams and from wells sunk near their houses. The population increase caused major sanitation and waste disposal problems, with reliance on cesspits in the gardens and waste thrown into the nearest stream. The new and old wells became polluted from nearby cesspits and cemeteries and outbreaks of disease were inevitable. Epidemics of typhoid, cholera, and diarrhoea were frequent. Infant mortality from water transmitted enteric disease was extremely high. Ill health from polluted water reduced the capacity of people to work. The following passage from a report by Dr John Snow in 1855 throws some light on the water quality available to communities only 140 years ago (Davey 1964):

These houses . . . were supplied by a copious spring in the road, the water of which was conducted to supply tanks behind each house . . . There was a cesspool behind each house under the privy and situated 4 feet from the water tank . . . The water was offensive and the deposit [in the tanks] possessed the odour of privy soil very distinctly . . . The people of Lower Fore Street obtained their water by dipping a pail into the Thames, there being no other supply.

The second half of the nineteenth century saw considerable investment in water treatment, in supply distribution systems and in sewage disposal. The first step was to construct sewers to take the sewage away from the houses but still to deposit it in the nearest river. Then it was realized that the water for drinking was coming from the river at places where the pollution from sewage discharges was making the water unfit for abstraction. So the next step was to introduce treatment for sewage before the water was returned to the river. An associated problem was that it had been the practice to spread sewage solids on the land to allow natural breakdown. In the absence of treatment this practice spread disease and made land unusable. Various forms of treatment involving agitation were tried and used. By the end of the century water supply distribution, sewer construction, and sewage removal and treatment meant that water-related disease was considerably reduced. Chlorine treatment to sterilize drinking water was generally adopted by 1920 and this substantially removed the remaining health risks.

It has to be realized that over this period Britain was an extremely wealthy country and could afford to invest in new technology and in widespread urban infrastructure.

The last fifty years

The resolution of major water-related health risks in Britain was a significant cause of the population increase. The population reached 37 million by 1900 and 49 million by 1950. Since then it has increased slowly and is almost stable at about 55 million. The end of the Second World War saw the development of agriculture and industry with renewed vigour and with them the signs of a range of water quality problems which have had to be addressed. There was a legacy of poor water quality in rivers, many of which were so polluted with industrial waste and sewage effluent that they were incapable of supporting animal and plant life. By increasing sewage treatment capacity, improving the techniques and controlling the discharges to rivers, wildlife has returned to many rivers. One famous example is the Thames, which was a dead river in 1900. By 1970 salmon were again found there and over a hundred species of fish could be caught in its waters.

Another problem arose from the intensification of agriculture. Farmers were encouraged to apply increased levels of chemical fertilizers to their crops to gain higher yields. Also they were offered a wide range of chemical controls for crop and animal pests. These substances were applied at levels which meant that large quantities increasingly found their way into water courses. The fertilizers, mainly nitrates and phosphates, caused algal blooms on rivers and lakes. The algae caused oxygen exhaustion in the water. The solution to the problem is to educate farmers to use fertilizers carefully, when the nutrients can be absorbed by the crops, and to take particular care to avoid water run-off containing fertilizers and pest chemicals from the land. It is also desirable to develop new crop growth methods and new plant varieties which do not need so much fertilizer and are more disease resistant, thus avoiding the use of pesticides.

The development of industry caused a significant increase in the discharge of heavy metals and this has had to be controlled through the adoption of discharge controls. It has to be said that whilst some improvements were achieved by this means the institutional arrangements in Britain were such that the controls were less effective than would be desirable. The institutional arrangements have been changed recently and are likely to be better at removing the flow of industrial pollution to water, air, and land.

John Bowman

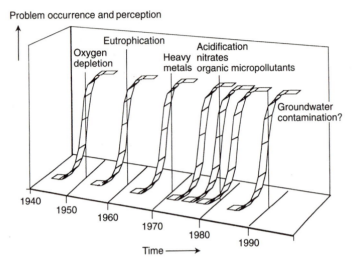

Problem occurrence and perception

Oxygen depletion

Eutrophication

Heavy metals

Acidification nitrates

organic micropollutants

Groundwater contamination?

1940 1950 1960 1970 1980 1990

Time ⟶

Fig. 4.4. Successive UK pollution issues. Source: Adapted from UNEP/WHO 1988.

The range of issues affecting the water industry in Western Europe has been fully categorized by UNEP/WHO 1988, from which Fig. 4.4 has been adapted to apply to the United Kingdom situation.

A SPECIAL CASE—EASTERN EUROPE

Countries of Eastern Europe have much the same history of development as Britain. The Romans included the area in their Empire and took with them the water technology that they used elsewhere. After the Empire collapsed, trade expanded and social change took place in these areas as in the rest of Europe. The growth of population fluctuated with the plagues, ports and towns grew and with them the problems of water supply and sanitation. This situation prevailed until well after the start of the Industrial Revolution in Western Europe. Whilst some industrialization took place, such as in the area which is now the Czech Republic, Eastern Europe remained a society more dependent on an agricultural economy even until the outbreak of the Second World War. More rural societies with less dense population pressures than in towns are not usually subject to as serious water supply and quality difficulties as urban areas.

In 1945, the forces of the Soviet Union entered Eastern Europe and the communist era began which was to last for the next 45 years. Though much of Eastern Europe and the Soviet Union remained rural, Stalin determined that the way forward lay in heavy industrialization and urbanization. At this stage Eastern Europe encountered the same water issues as Britain had addressed earlier in its history. The power for industrialization was produced from burning coal with a high sulphur content, from nuclear electricity stations, and from harnessing the hydro-energy on the big rivers. The water for the new urban areas, for industry and for new irrigated agricultural lands, was obtained by the construction of many new dams and by the diversion of major rivers. All these developments took place with scant regard for the environment. The prime and only objective was to raise the industrial output and income of the countries and to further the spread of communism to the rest of the world. Industrialization grew, with little regard for the health and safety of the population, and the technological methods were crude and relatively simple. As equipment and plant wore out there was little incentive to replace it with newer cleaner technology. The efficiency of the technology was low, using much more materials, energy, and labour than for comparable output and products in Western Europe. Little effort or investment was made in waste handling and the surrounding environment was used as the uncontained repository for anything of no immediate use. The outcome in water pollution terms was worse than anything experienced in Britain throughout the industrial period.

Since the fall of communism it has been possible to gauge

the full extent of environmental damage. Industry was mainly concentrated around large new cities, very often on the banks of large rivers. Whilst some legislation existed to set environmental standards and work practices, these were largely ignored. Controls on air and water emissions were ineffective or non-existent, and solid wastes, including nuclear waste and old radioactive plants, were dumped indiscriminately around the countryside. The diversion and harnessing for power generation of large rivers and inland seas was effected with little regard for the consequences for the environments previously dependent on the water. The outcome is that some rivers and lakes are drying up whilst in other areas badly managed irrigation has led to widespread salinization.

The air pollution, which can been seen and tasted by travellers to those countries, from coal-burning and metallurgical industries, is converted to acid rain containing heavy metals. Not only does this directly damage people who breathe the polluted air but health is impaired by poor water quality for municipal supply and by the ingestion of foods grown on contaminated soils and watered by the polluted rain. The dumped nuclear material has also found its way into water courses and into food crops. The result is that people in Eastern Europe and the former Sovet Union have some of the highest exposure to chemical pollutants and carcinogens in the world.

The new and old towns and cities have received little investment in infrastructure. Water supply and sewage disposal facilities are poorly constructed and maintained. Shortages of water are not uncommon and that which is supplied is often not fit to drink. Water and sewage treatment works are of inferior design and the ability and motivation of the staff is not good. Waste water from industry and from mining is discharged without treatment into adjacent water courses, leaving the water unfit even for industrial use.

Since the fall of the communist regimes the need to improve the supply and quality of water has been seen as a high priority for attention and new investment. The constraints on achieving the necessary action are formidable. Most of the economies are bankrupt and if industry and power stations are closed to reduce continuing pollution there will be no income to pay for the investment in water supply and treatment or indeed to feed the people. Huge sums of money are needed to clean-up the scattered waste material which is causing continuing pollution on water catchments and into rivers and lakes. There are severe problems associated with the technical capabilty of the staff and also with their willingness to take initiatives and responsibility. The communist system did not encourage anyone to be seen to be responsible. The institutional arrangements are an inhibition to change. For example, on the Volga river over eighty authorities have responsibility for managing the flow and use of the river. Though the new governments are paying much attention to water and environmental issues and drawing up new regulations, in many cases based on legislation in the European Community, there is still much antipathy to making the legislation effective by enforcement. This short account of the water problems facing Eastern Europe gives some indication of the difficulties which can occur in relatively advanced societies when industrialization proceeds without any regard for the sort of technology used and without control of irresponsible pollution by that industry. But the problem should not be blamed on industry alone. Rather it is a problem which arises from political failure and affects all aspects of society. It is a salutory lesson in what can go wrong and it should be recognized that a similar situation could arise in countries in the developing world where the damage could be at least as extensive if not more so.

FUTURE PROSPECTS

So far I have indicated that water is an essential requirement for life. It is used not only for drinking, personal hygiene, and sewage disposal but also for agriculture, industry, and recreation. In most parts of the world water is not being supplied in the quality and quantity required. The developing world experiences floods and droughts, leading to many deaths from drowning and from starvation. Even when water is available there are many deaths from water-related disease as a result of poor water, bad agricultural and industrial management, and through ignorance. This situation is set to become immeasurably worse as a consequence of the rising population, the inadequately planned and developed urban areas, and the growth of agriculture and industry. The question, 'Can disaster be avoided?', is not alarmist. A similar situation faced Europe in the past which we survived, but with a population which has almost ceased to expand and with very large investments in water storage and treatment. In the developed world there usually are sufficient safeguards in place to avoid many deaths from floods and droughts. By using clean and safe water supplies and by careful handling of sewage treatment and disposal, ill health and death from water-related disease have been reduced to relatively insignificant levels. However, there are still some such deaths and there are concerns that organic matter and chemical pollution are increasing and damaging currently clean water sources. The future even in the developed world has not been safeguarded satisfactorily.

In Eastern Europe since the fall of communism, it has become even clearer that the industrial practices in those countries has caused massive water pollution with radioactive materials and chemicals. The task to be faced there will be to change industrial practice to stop pollution at source and to find the resources to clean up the contaminated water sources and catchments. There are, therefore, large and widespread problems to be addressed if the objective of a sustainable future is to be achieved. So what can be done?

The developed world has learnt many lessons in the course of reaching the present situation where water-related disease and death are no longer major hazards. Whilst it does not have all the answers there is much advice it can offer to those less fortunate. Also, the developed world has the resources of education, research, and funding to help those who need and want it. Let us look again at the situation in the United Kingdom. The country has the benefit of a generally adequate rainfall distributed fairly evenly throughout the year. Periods of severe drought have been infrequent and floods have largely been contained. The need for water in different parts of the country does not match the local availability, so storage reservoirs and water transfer schemes have been built and more will be needed. In the south-east of the country, water supplies are mainly drawn from chalk aquifers which are affected by industrial and agricultural activities on the surface. In the north and west of the country where there is higher rainfall, supplies are drawn from surface reservoirs in which the water quality depends on the activities on the catchment, mainly farming and forestry. The main issues relating to water sources are as follows.

Conservation and storage of water from rainfall and snowmelt

A combination of natural ground-water reservoirs and man-made surface reservoirs is used to maintain the water supply. Even in the United Kingdom, because of the amount of water transpired by crops, there is no gain to storage from any precipitation which falls in the months April to October. The rainfall from October to April therefore has to supply the annual requirements. The amount which is stored depends not just on the size of the reservoir but also on the vegetation type on the catchment. It has been shown that because of the amount of evapotranspiration from trees, they reduce the yield of water from a catchment compared with grassland, particularly in lower rainfall porous soil areas. The vegetation affects the rate of run-off from the catchment and is important in determining the amount of water which can be transferred to storage.

Control of water quality by controlling ground use activites in the catchments

The fertilizer and agrochemical regime applied to crops on a catchment also affects the quality of the water. Nutrient enrichment will lead to algal and other plant growth, reducing the flow of water in the supply channels to the reservoirs and to the reduction of the oxygen level in the water. In areas

of intensive agriculture there is mounting concern that the
level of fertilizer applications, particularly nitrogen fertilizer,
is increasing the nitrogen level in the water sources above
the levels recommended by the World Health Organization.
Plant nutrients also reach ground water from the ploughing up
of long-established grassland and from the leakage of excreta
from livestock units such as dairies and piggeries. There are also
concerns at the levels of agrochemicals, particularly persistent
ones, used in the same areas, since these are increasing in
the underground sources. In consequence, schemes have been
introduced to pay farmers not to use fertilizers on areas where
water drains into underground aquifers. It may be that much
more restrictive agricultural practices will have to be encouraged
on water catchments.

Whilst agriculture and forestry use much of the land surface
in the storage catchments there are also other industries like
mining, metal working, chemical production, and tanning which
can leach pollutants into the ground water and reservoirs. These
need to be closely monitored and controlled.

Control of the discharges entering the catchment

Control of specific discharges to storage catchments must also
be regulated. Sewage effluent and industrial discharges are
important sources of water for re-use but also of organic
matter, chemicals, and possibly disease organisms. Fish farms,
particularly those operating within rivers, have been a growing
cause of concern as a source of nutrients from waste food and
faeces.

Control of atmospheric pollution

Mention was made earlier of the effect of air emissions from
power stations, industry, and motor vehicles leading to acid
rain and snow. It is essential that these emissions be modified
or reduced by altering the types of fuel used and by fitting
equipment to remove the oxides of sulphur and nitrogen from
the emissions.

The issues relating to sources of water have to be related to the issues relating to the systems for supply of water. Here there is a different range of matters, as follows.

Control of the location, and quantity of abstraction

The United Kingdom has operated for some years a system of licensing in order to control the place, time, and quantity of abstraction. Water is deemed to be a property of the state except in the case of some small abstraction sources on private property. Until recently the licence system has been inadequate for proper management of the water resource. The licences issued have not been properly related to the water available in the source; the quantities licensed for abstraction in some catchments have exceeded the total water available in the catchment. Fortunately, not all abstractors have taken their full entitlement but still many rivers throughout the country have dried up completely or for part of the year.

Irrigation in the United Kingdom is a relatively small user of water, but the timing of requirement comes when supplies are usually most scarce. Control on the time, method, and quantity of application is important, as well as encouragement of farmers to develop their own storage facilities specifically for irrigation. Other industries have been large users of water but the need is declining with the introduction of improved recycling processes and processes which use less water. Closed water systems involving zero discharge will find increasing favour.

Control the waste of water

In the United Kingdom it is estimated that up to 30 per cent of the municipal water supplied does not reach the end user because of leakages in the pipe system. The infrastructure is old and much of the pipework needs replacing, and this may be a cheaper alternative to finding additional sources of supply. Ensuring the distribution network is efficient is expensive but not usually more so than the cost of developing new supplies.

Several of the uses of water allow it to be used again for the same use or for another use. Cooling water from power stations, irrigation water, and water from sewage treatment works can be re-used after treatment. It is essential to ensure that such water returns to a catchment or river where it can be abstracted and that it is not allowed to flow to waste or the sea.

Control of sewage and industrial waste water disposal

The handling of sewage and other waste water is perhaps the most critical aspect of the water industry affecting human health. The controlled disposal of sewage to effective treatment works, together with improvements in personal hygiene, has been the major factor in disease control. The water closet, which has been in use since Roman times and probably much earlier, is effective but uses a lot of water. The design and adoption of toilets which use less water would make a major contribution to saving water needs.

The present system of mixing industrial effluents and sewage before treatment leads to complications in the design and operation of the treatment works. It would be desirable to separate the two types of discharge before treatment. Industrial waste waters would best be handled on site, thus reducing the movement of potentially dangerous substances. The separate treatment of mainly domestic sewage would be much simplified as a result. It would also be easier to dispose of sewage solids from the treatment process by incineration or by spreading on the land. Disposal to sea without complex treatment is not an option, in order to safeguard the quality of sea water for recreation.

Two other water-related subjects of current debate in the United Kingdom merit a brief mention because they have an important impact on the relation of water to health. One is the sort of institutional arrangements which should exist to manage the water industry.

The management of water conservation, treatment, and supply as well as the treatment and disposal of sewage and waste water disposal, can be effected either by private or public bodies.

However, it is quite clear that the monitoring of performance and the control of licences to abstract and to discharge waste water should be the responsibility of a different organization.

There may be a need for more than one regulator, as in the United Kingdom where there are at present three: one for environmental regulation, one for financial regulation where the suppliers are private sector monopolies, and one for product quality. It is also important for the regulators to have adequate authority to ensure that the law is observed.

The second subject relates to the cost of water. In the United Kingdom the water charge is based on the infrastructure, regulatory, and manpower costs of supplying the water. There is no cost for the basic resource itself, water. Water is seen as a public good to which everyone is entitled at minimal cost. This view of charging is now being questioned. It can be argued that a value should be placed on the resource, as an environmental asset which is lessened whenever the water is used. A higher cost for water would cause potential users to consider whether the use is essential or whether the same result can be achieved by other means using less water. It would lead to a more rational use of water and it would make people realize the need to treat water as a renewable resource only within limits. The cost of water in the United Kingdom has risen markedly in recent years and will rise still further in the years ahead as the cost of cleaning up past pollution and raising the standard of treatment works is passed on to the user.

For the developing world most of these issues are timely and pertinent. The means adopted to solve water problems in the United Kingdom may not be directly applicable elsewhere but the issues are the same ones to address if clean, sustainable water is to be available and if health is to improve. The United Kingdom has already experienced population growth, urbanization, and industrialization and has found the way to supply clean water and reduce water-related disease to a minor issue. The difficulty for the developing world is to find the resources of money and application to put the United Kingdom's experience to good use in the local situation.

There are, of course, some water problems in the developing world which are not found in the United Kingdom. One of these is the extent to which water is needed for irrigation. Growing populations will require more irrigated agriculture. Whilst some of this requirement can be met by more efficient use of water already used for irrigation, more water will have to be conserved and transferred from existing under-used sources.

A second major problem in the developing world is to control and reduce the vectors of water-borne disease, the mosquito and some species of snails and flies. Some of the chemical control methods may cause more health problems than they solve, if they get into water supplies for irrigation or for municipal use, and if the chemicals are toxic or cause cancer. Biological methods and changes in habitat management for the natural breeding grounds of the disease vectors are more appropriate controls.

The task of achieving sustainable water supplies in the developing world will not be easy and certainly one cannot be optimistic about the efforts currently being made. The rate of population growth and its associated social changes means that the difficulties of reducing water-associated disease are substantially greater than anything faced in Europe at a comparable stage of its development. The ultimate question is: Can the planet survive in its present form and yet support so many humans trying to attain the standard of living available to the relatively few living in the highly developed nations?

Finally, I return to the title of this paper. Water is best—would Pindar still think so? In the 2500 years since Pindar wrote those words, much has been learnt theoretically, and from experience, about the supply and quality of water and its effects on human health. Water supply still merits the priority for human life that Pindar's aphorism implies. However, the application of our accumulated wealth of knowledge leaves much cause for concern.

REFERENCES

Arar, A. (1987). Irrigation with sewage effluent: its application in the Near East Region (Western Asia). In *Water Quality Bulletin*, **12** (2), 51–8.

Bays, L. (1992). Urbanisation and birth rate thwart global water progress. In *Water Technology International 1992*, pp. 11–13. Century Press, London.

Chapman, D. (ed.) (1992). *Water quality assessments: a guide to the use of biota, sediments and water in environmental monitoring*. Chapman and Hall, London, for UNESCO/WHO/UNEP.

Davey, N. (1964). *Building in Britain—the growth and organisation of building processes in Britain from Roman times to the present day*. Evans Brothers, London.

Feachem, R. G., Bradley, D. J., Garelick, H., Mara, D. D. (1983). *Sanitation and disease: health aspects of excreta and wastewater management*, World Bank Studies in Water Supply and Sanitation *3*. Wiley, Chichester.

Frontinus, S. J. (1873). *The water supply of the city of Rome* (transl. C. Herschel). New England Water Works Association.

Ghali, B. B. (1992). Water management in the Nile Valley. In *Water Technology International 1992*, pp. 33–5. Century Press, London.

Kirkwood, G. (1982). *Selections from Pindar*. Scholars Press, Chico, CA.

Longworth, I. (1988). *Archaeology in Britain since 1945*. British Museum Publications, London.

Milaradov, M. (1990). Water resources of the Danube River Basin. *Water Science and Technology*, **22** (5), 1–12.

Nriagu, J. O. (1983). *Lead poisoning in antiquity*. Wiley, New York.

UNEP (1989). *Environmental data report 1989/90*. Blackwell, Oxford.

UNEP/WHO Global Environment Monitoring System (1988). *Assessment of freshwater quality*. Monitoring and Assessment Research Centre, London.

5

Health, environment, and tropical development

David Bradley

Professor David Bradley, DM, FRCP, FRCPath, FFCM, is one of the world's leading experts on tropical disease and its epidemiology. After training at University College Hospital Medical School and qualifying with First Class Honours, he went to Tanzania and for three years worked as a Medical Research Officer at the Ross Institute's Bilharzia Research Unit. In 1964 he took up an academic appointment at the Makerere University of East Africa, Uganda; he became a Senior Lecturer there in 1966. In 1969 Dr Bradley returned to the UK in order to take up a Royal Society Tropical Research Fellowship at the Sir William Dunn School of Pathology, Oxford University, which he held until 1973. After a year in the University's Clinical School of Medicine as Clinical Reader in Pathology, he was appointed to the Professorship of Tropical Hygiene at the University of London, and to the Directorship of the Ross Institute, in 1974 at the age of thirty-seven. He has held these posts ever since. Dr Bradley also holds a large number of honorary appointments and consultancies and has been a member of the World Health Organization's Advisory Panel on Parasitic Diseases for over twenty years. He edits the Journal of Tropical Medicine and Hygiene and has published four books on tropical disease as well as a large number of articles.

Nowhere has the environment so great and obvious an effect on health as in less developed countries, nor are there any countries where greater environmental changes are taking place as a result of the search, whether successful or otherwise, for socio-economic development. These environmental changes are in turn reflected in changes of health. Therefore environment and health cannot be usefully addressed without consideration of

Table 5.1 The possible interactions of health, environment, and development with examples

Possible interaction	Example
Environment favours development	Irrigated desert
Environment impedes development	Erosion of soils
Environment favours health	Better domestic water
Environment impedes health	Schistosomiasis in irrigation
Development favours health	Reduction of poverty
Development impedes health	Loss of land by the poor
Health favours development	Development of tea plantations
Health impedes development	Abandonment of agriculture
Development favours environment	Terracing of fields
Development impedes environment	Deforestation
Health favours environment	More energy to tackle problems
Health impedes environment	River blindness causing neglect

development; the interactions are complex and multidirectional, sometimes favourable and sometimes disastrous. Examples of twelve possible interactions are listed in Table 5.1 and shown diagrammatically in Fig. 5.1 (below).

In this chapter I survey the pattern and range of these interactions as they affect health, to see how the adverse effects may be averted, and point to the policy changes needed if health is to be optimized for any type of environmental change. It is first necessary to consider the concepts involved, particularly

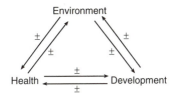

Fig. 5.1. Interactions of health, environment, and development.

that of 'environment', and to suggest an appropriate definition and ways to classify environment. There is a close connection between our concepts of health, environment, and development, and our perceptions of them; both aspects determine the actions taken to improve them.

Although definitions of health vary somewhat, depending on whether it is viewed as a positive state or merely the absence of disease, health has similar connotations for most of us. The same is true of development, although the range of opinion is greater. In contrast, environment tends to have a specific meaning for each person, and connotations may vary greatly between people. For one, environment is wilderness and wildlife, for another it involves pollution, and for yet another it concerns resources. All these are parts of the environment, and much confusion and bad policy may result from confusing parts with the whole. A comprehensive definition of environment is needed for health purposes, and that implied by the animal ecologists Andrewartha and Birch (1954) is the most appropriate: the environment of a person is everything outside him or her which directly or indirectly influences or is influenced by that person. Their taxonomy of the animal environment, which divides it into weather, food, a place to live, and other animals of the same and of different species, has much to commend it. This definition of the environment has the virtues of being broad and comprehensive. It is anthropocentric, as is essential in any real definition of the environment, as distinct from the world or the globe, because the concept of environment envisages a relationship between people and what is around them. The third advantage of this ecological definition of environment is that it envisages the environment as being that of an individual; Andrewartha and Birch (1954) would deny that there is an environment for a population. This has the advantage of viewing other people as part of the environment of an individual person, which perhaps puts the population questions relating to environment in their most appropriate place, although this last point is much more debatable than the others. A comparable subdivision of the human environment is as follows: ambience, which includes climate, radiation, and the like; food, including domestic water; habitat, or a place to live; other organisms, including other people and also pathogens such as bacteria and viruses (Bradley 1993*a*).

Views of environmental change differ between industrial and developing countries. In the former, there is a tendency to view past environments as Arcadia, provided that one goes back far enough in time (see Zehnder (1993) and other papers in Lake *et al.* (1993)). Such a naive or mythical view is untenable in developing countries, where environmental change may equally mistakenly be viewed as an aspect of socio-economic development. In fact, there will be diverse health changes, some beneficial and some detrimental. However, both collectively and individually they can be affected by modifying the nature of the environmental changes. It is also the case that many workers in developed countries focus on pollution as the key aspect of environmental change, whereas in developing countries depletion of local resources may loom larger, particularly under conditions of rapid population growth. Large changes in the habitat or place of living are apparent in both cases.

The starting point for health in an African, Asian, or Latin American village will be grim. In parts of Malawi where holoendemic malaria is superimposed on diarrhoeas and respiratory infections, up to 40 per cent of children may fail to reach their fifth birthday, and Mata (1978) has graphically shown the massive burden of environmentally determined disease that affects those Guatemalan children who do survive. The child may scarcely gain any weight between six and thirty-six months of age. The two main causes of such health problems in the least developed countries are malnutrition and infections. Infections in developing countries can be ascribed to two broad causal factors: poverty and a warm climate. A warm temperature allows animal parasites (protozoa and helminths) to complete the essential part of their life cycle outside man, while the complex of social and environmental factors that comprise poverty facilitate the transmission of very many infections.

Environmental change away from this burden of disease

may occur as a result of deliberate environmental engineering to improve health (what is commonly called 'environmental health' in a narrow sense—the realm of the environmental health officer, formerly the sanitary inspector) or as a side-effect of activities aimed at socio-economic development, such as water resource development or industrialization. These may affect health directly, as a result of environmental change altering disease transmission or health risk, or indirectly by affecting the disposable income of the inhabitants (Fig 5.2). A hydroelectric dam and reservoir may create habitats for the snails that transmit schistosomiasis but destroy those of the blackflies that spread river blindness. It may also impoverish those displaced from their farms and sources of income by the rising waters whilst enriching those who use the electricity to improve their economic activities. The distinction becomes relevant even at the planning stage of any environmental change, because developments that affect the distribution of disposable income amongst the population remain the responsibility of economic planners. It is desirable to prevent equity in economic development from being delegated to the health sector and conveniently forgotten.

Since the relations between environmental change and health are so complex, development projects give rise to both problems and opportunities. Whilst it is crucial at the planning stage to avoid making the environment more conducive to disease (Weil *et al.* 1990), it is also important to determine what

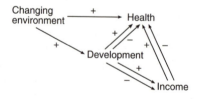

Fig. 5.2. The consequences of deliberate environmental change aimed at either health or development.

opportunities can be utilized to improve health. Where change is concerned, the boundaries between the physical environment, the socio-economic environment, and human behaviour are closely interrelated. Thus it is no use putting in a supply of better quality drinking water if no one makes the necessary adjustments in their behaviour to use it; more extensive environmental changes inevitably require that the inhabitants of an area adopt a different pattern of life (Feachem *et al.* 1983).

In the following sections many of these themes will be illustrated in terms of the interactions between water and health, since water plays a particularly important role as an aspect of the environment affecting health (Bradley 1977). The discussion focuses especially upon infections because, on a world scale, it is the communicable diseases related to water which greatly exceed in importance the chemical problems of water pollution. Water shows clearly the relation between our taxonomy of an environmental change, the concepts we apply, and public policy. The water-related infections of man are extremely numerous and diverse. A classification related to their biological nature into viruses, bacteria, protozoa, etc. leads to a complex biological classification from which it is not easy to move towards environmental health issues. In contrast, if we use an intervention-linked taxonomy with an epidemiological basis, the prospects for improvement can be analysed and become much clearer. The situation globally is more complex than that in the UK where the quality of domestic water tends to be the main concern of those addressing the health problems related to water. In the tropics water supply is a resource issue, not just one of pollution, and it can be shown that increasing the availability of water even without improving its bacteriological quality may significantly improve health. We can replace the complex biological classification by a relatively simple system in terms of environmental interventions related to epidemiology (White *et al.* 1972). There are four ways in which disease may be related to water. In the first, the pathogenic organisms are transmitted from one person to another through their domestic water supply. The second category includes those diseases whose transmission is reduced when the supply of water is more readily available. Such infections include many of the diarrhoeal diseases, and infections of the skin and eyes which are reduced when the supply of water is adequate for personal cleanliness. They are conveniently grouped together as the 'water-washed' diseases. A third group of infections are those transmitted by organisms which live in water. The schistosome worms develop in aquatic snails, and the guinea worm parasite, which causes so much misery in Africa and India, develops in minute crustacea which live in wells and other bodies of water. The parasites may gain access to people from the water either by being swallowed in the case of guinea worm, or by boring their way through the skin as occurs with schistosomiasis. Because their intermediate hosts are based in the water, these are conveniently called the 'water-based' diseases. A fourth category comprises infections transmitted by insect vectors which are related in some way to water. All the mosquitoes have larvae which develop in water; some species of tsetse flies, although they develop in the soil, will only bite near water. Therefore these comprise the diseases with 'water-related insect vectors'. Above all this category includes malaria and the arthropod-borne viruses (arboviruses) such as yellow fever.

DOMESTIC WATER AND SANITATION

This is the traditional area of health improvement by deliberate environmental change. It is undertaken by public health engineers whose intellectual background until relatively recently had been firmly based in the problems of industrialized countries. Exploration of broader issues in tropical water supply, originally by field studies at many sites throughout East Africa (White *et al*. 1972), has led to a change of emphasis in relation to developing countries. First, there are more choices for the user than was generally perceived. The alternatives are not simply between a totally unimproved shallow well and filtered chlorinated water delivered to multiple taps within a dwelling;

rather, there are a whole series of partial interventions between these two extremes. Exploration of the very diverse literature suggests that the majority of health benefits can be achieved with a domestic water supply of between 30 and 50 litres per head per day. To achieve this something more than water carried from the source is usually needed, and the ready availability of domestic water is more important than very large volumes. The evidence suggests quite strongly that the provision of a single tap is required to achieve the available health benefits, and a flow-limiting device may be fitted to minimize the peak flow which determines the scale of pipes needed. With a regular rainfall there are alternative solutions such as the use of rain-water cisterns. The most cost-effective methods of obtaining adequate water supplies are very locationally specific. There are often simple interventions which are highly appropriate for a particular situation, but quite sophisticated understanding is required in order to advise on which will be the most successful. Even though improved supplies of less than perfectly safe water may increase health substantially, engineers have been very reluctant to become involved in such schemes because of their relatively rigid professional training. Understandably, professionals are also unwilling to design pipes which may bring water which may make some people ill closer to the house, even though the resulting illness is far less than would be the case if no improvements were made.

A further change in thinking that has occurred in recent decades is from the previously accepted wisdom that governments should build water supplies and communities maintain them, to a realization that the reverse is more often likely to be successful. It is relatively easy during an agriculturally slack season to encourage villagers to work enthusiastically on the construction of a much needed water supply for a week or so, but the problems of maintenance, of storing spare parts over many years, and of being able to produce the right part at short notice are much more suited to a bureaucracy than to the functioning of a village.

This central problem of the long-term maintenance of environmental changes necessary for health will recur. The funding of environmental change, usually by outside development banks, means that the most able staff are attracted into the excitement of construction projects, whereas the scarce recurrent expenditure is spread very thinly and inadequately for the less glamorous purposes of operation and maintenance. A consequence of this is that many environmental changes consist of short dramatic periods of construction and then progressive slow, or not so slow, decay until it is decided either to replace the project or rehabilitate it so massively that it bears little resemblance to the original undertaking. These issues commonly affect environmental changes that influence health.

CONTROL OF VECTOR-BORNE DISEASE

Until the availability of DDT after 1940 and of molluscicides after 1950, the only methods of controlling transmission of vector-borne diseases in developing countries were environmental. Although such environmental management went back to the mists of antiquity with the draining of marshes for agricultural purposes, it was only undertaken in a specific and rational manner following the demonstration of the mosquito transmission of malaria at the beginning of this century. It soon became apparent that different species of anopheline mosquito were responsible for malaria transmission in different areas, and that each species had precise requirements in terms of breeding site. Thus one species might only breed in very shallow water that was extensively shaded, while another might prosper in gently running streams in open sunlight. The work of Watson in Malaysia and of Swellengrebel in Indonesia fully exploited this habitat specificity of mosquitoes, and over the years they developed methods of modifying the habitat to exclude specific species of anophelines, a practice known as species sanitation. Sometimes this was done on a small scale. At the other extreme, in the Tennessee Valley Authority, methods were developed of putting siphons into the dams of reservoirs so that the whole reservoir level could be lowered by several feet weekly, thus stranding the larvae of mosquitos breeding round the edge. The profession of malaria engineer evolved during this period. One of the main effects of the discovery of DDT was to render most thinking about environmental control temporarily obsolete, so that a major problem of the last two decades has been to try and rediscover much of what was known by that earlier generation.

New environmental approaches to species sanitation have been developed. The most successful, and one of the least expensive, has been the use of small polystyrene spheres to cover the surface of static polluted water in order to prevent the breeding of *Culex quinquefasciatus*, which is the vector of elephantiasis and is also a nuisance mosquito on an immense scale in the great tropical cities. In Dar es Salaam and Zanzibar, for instance, much breeding takes place in flooded pit latrines owing to the combination of a high water table and the extensive use of such latrines, even in urban areas. A layer of polystyrene spheres floating on the top of the flooded pit latrine prevents the mosquito larvae from having access to air and thus causes them to die. It has been found that the layer of polystyrene beads lasts up to seven or more years and thus is highly cost effective. There are no environmental effects as long as the beads remain in the latrine. Another recent development has been the use of insecticides to impregnate bed nets. The resulting protection provided by impregnated bed nets against malaria transmission is very great since it combines reduction of biting with shortening the life of the vectors. Only small quantities of insecticide are used, and it is of a less persistent type than DDT.

CLIMATIC CHANGE AND VECTOR-BORNE DISEASE

Although global climatic change is one of the more frequently discussed aspects of environmental change, it is probably much less important than the other changes considered in this chapter as far as the transmission of communicable disease is concerned. Nevertheless, global warming is likely to have both indirect effects on health by way of agriculture, since changes in temperature and humidity are likely to have extensive effects on the growth of crops, and also more directly through the breeding and survival of insect vectors of disease (Sutherst 1993). Because there is great uncertainty on the likely changes in humidity, and it is the combination of temperature and humidity which affects mosquito breeding and survival, it is very difficult to make sound predictions of the likely effects on vector-borne disease except for one aspect. This is the duration of the extrinsic cycle: the time between the infection of an insect with a parasite such as that causing malaria and the first day on which it is able to pass on the infection to others. The duration of the extrinsic cycle is temperature dependent, and is around ten to twelve days for malaria in many of its vectors. Calculations have shown that a rise in temperature of two degrees can very greatly increase malaria transmission, up to a hundredfold, at the lower end of the range within which malaria can be transmitted (Bradley 1993*b*). Other effects of global climatic change on vector-borne disease are highly speculative. The effect of shortening the extrinsic cycle is likely to be most apparent in mountainous tropical areas, where one would expect the altitudinal limits to malaria transmission to increase. Since these areas are usually heavily populated, the potential for epidemic outbreaks of malaria is very great. The latitudinal limits of malaria are rather rarely determined purely by issues of temperature and humidity. Humans already play a much larger role, but in the Asian republics of the former USSR latitudinal extension of the range of malaria is more likely because of climatic effects.

WATER RESOURCE DEVELOPMENTS

Among the habitat changes deliberately produced to achieve socio-economic development, the development of water resources is probably the most important for health. The last few decades have been characterized by extensive construction of dams and reservoirs for hydroelectric purposes, to feed irrigation schemes, or to stabilize the flow of rivers. They are undertaken for development rather than health purposes, but may have serious adverse consequences for health (Stanley and Alpers 1975). Reservoirs usually replace more rapidly flowing streams and thus convert torrential water previously suitable for the development of the insect vectors of river blindness into calm waters more appropriate for the development of schistosomiasis in water snails. In many tropical areas there will also be an increase of malaria, although this usually will not apply in Africa where transmission is already at a very high level in the absence of water resource development (Macdonald 1955; Bradley 1991*a*).

Water resource developments exhibit several features common to many environmental changes but in a particularly complex form. Not only does the environment change but also people move. Clearly, when a dam is created there is planned evacuation of those living in the area where the reservoir will be located, but there are usually larger-scale unplanned movements, characteristically of fishermen from far and wide, to the new lake which may initially have a very high fish productivity. During the construction phase of any large dam there will be a large immigrant population, usually with consequences for the incidence of trauma, venereal disease and other such accompaniments of the aggregation of temporary labour (Bradley 1977). In the case of a large dam there will also be a substantial immigrant expatriate population, either of foreign nationals or of people from the capital city with professional qualifications, who may be totally unaccustomed to living in the wilds. The demands of this group for a high level of health care may be put to good use for the long term. There is the opportunity to build health care facilities which, once the dam is fully constructed, can be used by the residents of the area. It may also provide the opportunity to bring in environmental health measures to control the variety of locally prevalent diseases. Because of the complexity of the changes in environment and health there is a great tendency for the literature to be highly biased, either viewing a new dam as a great economic boon or alternatively as the source of many evils. In reality life is far more complicated, and any water resource development will contain a mixture of changes which can both benefit and be deleterious to health. What is generally clear is that thoughtful planning prior to the construction phase can minimize the health problems at least cost. The distribution of costs and benefits among the population usually raises many problems which affect health. Those displaced from the reservoir site are almost invariably much worse off economically and in every other way, despite efforts being made to resettle them and to provide them with new work. In contrast, the main benefits are likely to accrue to people far distant from the site of the environmental change.

The long duration of the secular changes that take place once a reservoir is constructed is not generally appreciated. In the case of a large dam a steady state may not be reached for 15 or more years. When Lake Volta was constructed in Ghana there was initial flooding of forested land, decay of the trees led to eutrophication of the lake waters, and the insects that were eating the rotten wood were in turn consumed by a vast number of fish so that catches from the lake rose to the order of 40 000 tonnes per annum. Vast numbers of fisherman moved in. The eutrophication also led to a great increase of water-weed, providing an extensive snail habitat so that *Bulinus truncatus rolfsi* proliferated greatly and acted as an extremely efficient intermediate host for schistosomiasis.

After some years the trees had all completely disintegrated, the insect populations declined and therefore so did fish; and the water ceased to have the same degree of eutrophication so that the water-weed levels decreased and hence the snail populations declined. Even after 15 years secular changes were still taking place in the biology of the system. As the majority of research studies tend to be on a three year horizon, such long-term changes in epidemiology tend to be little studied and are poorly documented. It is interesting that in the Gezira

irrigation scheme of the Sudan in the 1930s there was a schistosomiasis problem which was due to *Schistosoma haematobium*
carried by one group of water snails. By the 1970s there was still
a severe schistosomiasis problem but the species had changed,
and *Schistosoma mansoni*, transmitted by a quite different genus
of snails, predominated. Currently there is a swing back to *S.
haematobium*. We do not know the reason for this and the
problem is not very tractable.

The shoreline of Lake Volta is very irregular and extends
for many thousands of kilometres. Snails are present all along
the periphery, but transmission of schistosomiasis only occurs
where there is close contact between people and water. The
majority of transmissions take place at one or two sites per
lakeshore village, at the points where canoes are beached and
unloaded, where water contact is very high. The same places
are often used for domestic water collection. The interaction
between environmental change and behaviour is clearly seen.

Similar problems, particularly involving schistosomiasis, occur
in irrigation schemes. Here the transmission takes place in the
slow-flowing drains which are used to remove excess water from
the irrigated area. Canals tend to be better maintained than
drains because people are concerned to obtain enough water
for their land, whereas the problems of water logging and
saline accumulation are less immediately apparent. Frequently,
villagers are left to rely upon a canal or more usually one of the
distributary canals which, instead of being only intermittently
filled with water, are kept permanently filled to provide a village
water supply. This combines static water with a high level of
human water contact and makes for massive transmission of
schistosomiasis. It is notable that in The Gambia methods of
schistosome control using medical treatment of people at regular
intervals completely failed in two villages, which were the two
using tributaries of a river as their water supply rather than wells
and seasonal pools.

The adverse health effects of water resource developments
are best handled at the design stage of the dam or irrigation
scheme and when the detailed planning of settlements and

of construction procedures is under way (Tiffen 1991). The practical problem is that engineers are usually in charge of design and until recently have tended to focus very sharply on the main economic purpose of the water resource development, whether it was hydroelectric power generation or irrigation water management, and have been reluctant to allocate significant sums to other matters of human welfare. Matters have improved considerably, particularly in large irrigation schemes where the funding usually comes from international sources. Environmental concern in such agencies as the World Bank means that an environmental impact assessment (EIA) has to be carried out for each project that will produce significant changes in the habitat. Even more crucially, the person who drafts the original terms of reference of the project is in a key position to ensure that health aspects are taken seriously. If they appear in the terms of reference, then the consulting engineers and others who may become involved will make provision to deal with the issues. If they are merely a pious hope and expressed in general documents, then they will have much less impact. The concept of environmental impact assessment preceded ordinary health issues in the concerns of many lending agencies. Therefore the World Bank, which set an example in these matters, considered health change as a side-effect of environmental impact in relation to water resource developments and focused almost entirely upon schistosomiasis. The result was that in some irrigation schemes very substantial investments were made to prevent the schistosomiasis situation becoming worse as a result of the water resource development, but the expenditure on that was wholly disproportionate to the expenditure on the other health needs of the population. The sequence by which environmental impact assessment leads on to health or environmental health impact assessment is less than optimal from a health viewpoint. We would argue that a specific health opportunity assessment (HOA) should be part of any substantial development of water or land resources. To look only at certain diseases is a very narrow approach and may well lead to interventions which are not cost effective. The concept of a HOA, originally suggested two years ago (Bradley 1991*b*), has been taken up by several of the international agencies through the Panel of Experts on Environmental Management (a joint World Health Organization/Food and Agricultural Organization of the United Nations/United Nations Environmental Programme/United Nations Human Settlements Programme) which has developed courses around it. If the purpose of development is to increase the total sum of human welfare, then health is worthy of consideration in any significant programme that involves environmental change.

In contrast with the improving situation in the case of large dams and irrigation schemes, the situation around small water resource developments remains extremely unsatisfactory. Small dams are very much more numerous than large ones, so that in a country such as Nigeria with one large dam at Kainji there may also be more than 500 small dams in a single state within the country. These dams do not involve international funding; they are often undertaken by local agriculturalists or entrepreneurs or the local government in a relatively unplanned manner. They affect the lives of a far larger number of people in aggregate than do the large dams, and it is very unusual for health considerations to be taken seriously in their planning, construction, or subsequent fate. From a research viewpoint they are more tractable than the large developments, partly because there are many of them, and methods of disease control worked out in relation to a few can be applied to a much larger number, whereas studies of large dams find rather few consumers within the same country simply because of the small number of large dams in any one country. However, the difficulties of implementing any conclusions are very substantial.

Perhaps the most expensive form of water resource development practised in any country is that of polderization: the building of large dams to restrict flooding of large areas of low-lying land and to transform the water regime over that area of land. The Netherlands are pre-eminent in the engineering and other aspects of polderization because their country has depended upon it for its existence. Currently Bangladesh is undertaking polderization of vast areas, and this consumes a very substantial part of the foreign aid to the country. Remarkably, the consequences of polderization have received little investigation and only now are beginning to attract attention. The changes in water regime have complex effects upon the transmission of such diseases as cholera as well as producing complex redistribution of income since, for example, people can no longer use small hand-propelled boats for transport and the role of lorries and other forms of road transport becomes much greater. The overall epidemiological consequences of these changes are poorly understood, despite the vast sums of money expended on the actual construction of embankments.

FORESTS

The destruction of tropical rainforests has become a major concern of environmental conservationists. The epidemiological consequences of changes in forest cover have been of concern for well over a century, and our understanding of diseases transmissible between other vertebrate animals and man, the zoonoses, has arisen from epidemiological work by Russian research workers during the colonization of the Siberian forests and parts of Soviet Central Asia. They observed that such diseases as Russian spring/summer encephalitis were associated with settlements in the forest where people came into contact with ticks which normally transmitted the lethal virus between a variety of wild mammals. When humans came up against the forest edge or lived in small clearings in the forest, they were exposed to a new environment which was associated with a particular range of new diseases. The Russian workers developed the subject as a whole into a new discipline called landscape epidemiology. Two decades later Audy (1968) drew attention to the epidemiology of scrub typhus in Malaysia. This was transmitted by mites, and again occurred in a situation where people were coming into contact with the edge of the forest. The same has been true of leishmaniasis and malaria among those who constructed the trans-Amazon highway in Brazil, and continues to be a problem for settlers within the Amazon region.

The ecologically unstable edges between two environments, called ecotones, are often sites for transmission of the zoonoses. People who are the inhabitants of one environment come into contact with insect and arthropod vectors of disease from alternative environments which are then able to carry over infections from the forest to the plains. This is perhaps most clearly seen in the case of jungle yellow fever where the vertical migrations of mosquitoes between the canopy inhabited by non-human primates and the forest floor invaded by wood collectors and others may be the origin of human cases of yellow fever transmitted in Africa by the mosquito *Aedes africanus*. At the edge of the forest the transmission may be continued by *Aedes simpsoni* which lives in regenerating forest edges and agricultural land adjacent to forests. This may lead to more cases of yellow fever. If those who are infected then come into settlements and urban areas where *Aedes aegypti*, the classical vector of yellow fever, is prevalent, massive person-to-person epidemics may take place. Therefore the forest edge may act as a reservoir of many infections. In Asia and Brazil there are further problems due to malaria transmitted by forest-dwelling mosquitoes, which in both cases happen to be extremely efficient vectors. *Anopheles dirus* in the forest fringes of South and Southeast Asia and *Anopheles darlingi* in the Amazon Basin are responsible for substantial epidemics of malaria amongst those who are cutting down the forest and settling near the edge of the canopy. When the forest has been totally destroyed for a long way around then the level of malaria in these two areas may decrease, but clearly this is a very unsatisfactory solution to the problem!

More complex environmental changes, especially where there is deliberate interference with the local vegetation, may lead to wholly unexpected health consequences. The classic example is the introduction of *Lantana camera* to Kenya. Because of its rapid transpiration, this plan had been successfully used in

Malaysia to dry out swamps, thus leading to a reduction in malaria vectors. An agricultural officer ill-advisedly felt that *Lantana* would be a less noxious plant than the *Euphorbia* used for field hedges in areas of the Alego District in Western Kenya. Unfortunately the humidity within *Lantana* bushes is extremely high and this enabled *Glossina fuscipes*, a species of tsetse fly which normally fed on humans only by forested lake edges, to leave the lake shore and live peridomestically in the *Lantana* hedges, thus leading to a brisk and serious epidemic of sleeping sickness in which over 600 people were infected with this usually fatal disease.

URBANIZATION

As demonstrated above, ecotones are very often the site of major health problems. The rapid growth of cities leads to accumulation of poor immigrants in the urban areas around their peripheries. Often, the infrastructure of cities was designed in the past when they were much smaller. It provides relatively good environmental health for an official sector and for residences for the officials, which are also near the centre, with transfer of problems of waste disposal to the area immediately around the city which is becoming heavily populated by the poor. It could be said as a generalization that pollution tends to spread while resources tend to cluster, and the migrants to the city tend to inhabit this septic fringe where resources are limited but pollution is abundant, not only from their activities but often transferred from the centre of the city. Under these circumstances one obtains a combination of the diseases of underdevelopment (the classical tropical diseases, and other infections) together with those of development, so that people have a high prevalence of communicable diseases and also suffer substantial mortality from cardiovascular diseases and cancer. Malnutrition will be common and pollution will lead to the proliferation of some disease vectors and also to the problems of inorganic pollution associated with industrialization. The level of poverty also means that industry does not control its own polluting activities to the degree which can be enforced in richer communities. In many tropical cities the classical environmental health problems of water supply and sanitation are particularly acute, as is the problem of surface water drainage. In some communities imaginative methods have been brought to bear upon methods of human waste disposal, and various low cost methods of vector control and waste disposal have been developed.

The health problems of socio-economic development and its associated environmental changes have been illustrated by the problems of forest edges, the edges of water bodies and irrigation schemes, and the edges of cities. Urban development today tends to involve very large populations. This is in marked contrast with the situation in, for example, the city states of Renaissance Italy where a high degree of development was possible but in relatively small communities. Many of today's problems are due to very high human population densities. There has been much recent debate about the concept of carrying capacity as applied to human environments. Sufficient empirical evidence is being gathered to show that the situation is neither simple nor straightforward. A dramatically counter-intuitive example has been revealed by the work of Tiffen (1993) and Tiffen and Mortimore (1992) in the Machakos area of Kenya where a situation of gross environmental degradation associated with overpopulation was very carefully documented in the late 1930s. It was a very clear example of the currently orthodox view of the situation. However, remarkably, when the area was re-studied recently, the environment had been put into very good order and was well cared for even though the population density was five times greater than in the 1930s. In other words, there is no simple relationship between population density and environmental degradation. This single example should not be overemphasized, but it does illustrate the extreme complexity of the relationships. What is quite clear is that in large cities, to which people migrate with hopes of employment and a better life, there is a lack of environmental resources and also a need for public health measures. While there are low cost methods of controlling the breeding of vectors in dirty water, it is also true that in the absence of a reliable water supply water will have to continue to be stored by individuals, and that small and medium-sized containers provide an admirable breeding habitat for the mosquitoes which are the vectors of yellow fever and dengue.

However, there are extremely positive aspects of the current scene. They are epitomized by the situation in a village in Thailand where the monks in the village monastery, encouraged by the abbot, developed a biogas plant for the digestion of human and animal wastes with the production of methane. This had the practical consequence that people cleaned up the environment and the village in order to put the waste into the methane digester. Perhaps even more important was the conceptual leap from viewing excreta as a waste product to viewing it as a resource for the generation of methane in sufficient quantities to heat the rice for the meals of the monks and others. Once a product is viewed as a resource rather than a waste product, it becomes much easier to formulate rules for dealing with it and for its intelligent and safe use. It is clear that the high temperatures found in the tropics, though they may have disadvantages for food storage, make appropriate many low cost technologies which are capable of rendering waste safe for use and which can be operated on a local scale. In turn, the use of these technologies leads to behavioural changes. The ways in which these technological changes can be most appropriately carried out in a given area requires deep understanding not only of the environment and the changes occurring in it and of health, but also of the culture, the economy, and the population.

CONCLUSIONS

It can be concluded that environment is a major determinant of disease in developing countries, even more than in industrialized countries; that environmental change is inevitable because of the pressures of population, the needs of people, and their hopes for a better life; and that these changes may lead to an increase in some diseases and a decrease in others. It is possible for us, the world's inhabitants, to determine the nature, speed, and direction of these environmental changes and to plan them in such a way that they will be relatively successful in the improvement of human health, but this will require hard thinking and difficult, often politically unpopular, actions in the short run if we are to obtain sustainable improvements in health. There are no easy answers, and only a very limited number of 'quick fixes' are likely to be discovered. Those of us who live in industrial and relatively rich countries have far more power to determine the direction of these environmental changes than the poor inhabitants of the least developed countries. But to do so and to make the right decisions at all levels requires research at the biological, medical, and social levels as well as deep environmental understanding which in turn will require much research. It also requires forethought, planning, and political commitment. The random interaction of market forces is not sufficient to prevent environmental degradation. Planning itself will not have any effect unless it is effectively implemented, which has both political and practical connotations. It is possible with sufficient thought and determination to produce a better environment which is conducive to good health as well as to socio-economic development. Prevention, or at the very least early action, is better and often cheaper in the long run than cure, or than coping with or simply suffering the health consequences of environmental change. Overseas aid can be a positive force in this respect, although it is not always the case, and it can help those who wish to take a long-term view. EIA helped to bring the problems to people's notice, but HOA is much better and more proactive and seeks opportunities for action and then to make them a component of the environmental change related to socio-economic development. Research, planning, commitment, and effective action are all needed if we are to have an environment which is conducive to health as well as to the other necessities for human life.

REFERENCES

Andrewartha, H. G. and Birch, L. C. (1954). *The distribution and abundance of animals*. University of Chicago Press.

Audy, J. R. (1968). *Red mites and typhus*. Athhlone Press, London.

Bradley, D. J. (1977). The health implications of irrigation schemes and man-made lakes in tropical environments. In *Water, wastes and health in hot climate countries* (ed. R. G. Feachem, M. G. McGarry, and D. D. Mara), pp. 18–29 Wiley, New York.

Bradley, D. J. (1991*a*). Malaria. In *Disease and mortality in sub-Saharan Africa* (ed. R. G. Feachem and D. T. Jamison), pp. 201–43. Oxford University Press for the World Bank.

Bradley, D. J. (1991*b*). Malaria—whence and whither. In *Malaria: waiting for the vaccine* (ed. G. A. T. Targett), pp. 11–29. Wiley, Chichester.

Bradley, D. J. (1993*a*). Environmental aspects of public health in developing countries. *Atti dei Convegni Lincei*, **102**, 85–95.

Bradley, D. J. (1993*b*). Human tropical diseases in a changing environment. In *Environmental change and human health* (ed. J. V. Lake, G. R. Bock, and K. Ackrill), Ciba Symposium 175, pp. 146–70. Wiley, Chichester.

Feachem, R. G., Bradley, D. J., Garelick, H., and Mara, D. D. (1983). *Sanitation and disease: health aspects of excreta and waste water management*. Wiley, Chichester.

Lake, J. V., Bock, G. R., and Ackrill, K. (eds.). (1993). *Environmental change and human health*, Ciba Symposium 175. Wiley, Chichester.

Macdonald, G. (1955). Medical implications of the Volta River project. Transactions of the Royal Society of Tropical Medicine and Hygiene, **49**, 13–24.

Mata, L. J. (1978). *The children of Santa Maria Cauqué: a prospective field study of health and growth*. MIT Press, Cambridge, MA.

Stanley, N. F. and Alpers, M. P. (ed.) (1975). *Man-made lakes and human health*. Academic Press, London.

Sutherst, R. W. (1993), Arthropods as disease vectors in a changing environment. In *Environmental change and human health* (ed. J. V. Lake, G. R. Bock, and K. Ackrill.), Ciba Symposium 175, pp 124–45. Wiley, Chichester.

Tiffen, M. (1991). *Incorporation of health safeguards into irrigation projects through intersectoral cooperation* (2nd edn.). PEEM Secretariat, World Health Organization, Geneva.

Tiffen, M. (1993). Productivity and environmental conservation under rapid population growth: a case study of Machakos District. *Journal of International Development*, **5**, 207–23.

Tiffen, M. and Mortimore, M. (1992). Environment, population growth and productivity in Kenya: a case study of Machakos District. *Development Policy Review*, **10**, 359–87.

Weil, D. E. C., Alicbusan, A. P., Wilson, J. F., Reich, M. R., and Bradley D. J. (1990). *The impact of development policies on health*. World Health Organization, Geneva.

White, G. F., Bradley, D. J., and White, A. U. (1972). *Drawers of water*. University of Chicago Press.

Zehnder, A. J. B. (1993). River Rhine: from sewer to the spring of life. In *Environmental change and human health* (ed. J. V. Lake, G. R. Bock, and K. Ackrill, K.), Ciba Symposium 175, pp. 42–61. Wiley, Chichester.

6

Changing diseases in changing environments

Robert May

Professor Robert May, FRS, is Royal Society Research Professor in the Department of Zoology of the University of Oxford and at Imperial College London. He graduated at the University of Sydney, where he also took his doctorate, in theoretical physics in 1959. He lectured in applied mathematics at Harvard University for two years before returning to Sydney in 1962 to take up the post of Senior Lecturer in Theoretical Physics; he was promoted to a Readership in 1964 and awarded a Personal Chair in 1969. In 1973, Professor May returned to the USA on his appointment to the Professorship of Biology at Princeton University, where he also held the Class of 1877 Professorship of Zoology. He took up his Research Professorship at Oxford in 1988. Professor May is the author of numerous books and articles on both epidemiology and ecology. He was awarded the Linnean Medal in 1991.

INTRODUCTION

Death from infectious disease was a much more commonplace thing in Victorian Britain than it is today. Most readers of this book will be able to cast their minds back several generations in their own family history to recall how the large families of Victorian times typically lost several children before adulthood. Likewise, children often lost parents—not least that symbol of the Victorian Age, Prince Albert—to infectious diseases. Such events run through the literature of that age: Beth in *Little Women*, the eponymous and obnoxiously saintly *Little Lord Fauntleroy*, the *Lady of the Camellias*.

As late as the 1930s, a typical ward of a large city hospital in the developed world would have been populated mainly with patients with pneumonia, meningitis, typhoid fever, endocarditis, mastoiditis, syphilis, tuberculosis, rheumatic fever, and various bacteraemias. There were few effective therapies for these infectious diseases, and most of the patients—many of them young—would die of the disease or its complications. In contrast, the wards of such a hospital today are filled with patients with non-communicable diseases such as cancer, heart disease, or the complications of diabetes or hypertension.

This change in the disease patterns in developed countries owes much to the development of antibiotics during and after the Second World War, and later to the development and widespread use of vaccines. It has prompted many to see the ravages of infectious diseases as a thing of the past. This view is typified by the triumphalist testimony of the US Surgeon General to Congress in 1969 that it was time to 'close the book on infectious diseases' (quoted by Bloom and Murray 1992). Such triumphalism is grievously in error, for at least three reasons.

First, the apparent victory over infectious diseases has never been won outside the developed world. While it is true that contemporary survivorship curves (curves showing the probability to live to a given age) in developed countries indeed confirm that most of us can expect to attain the promised three score years and ten, the corresponding survivorship curves in Third World countries are very different. In fact, these curves are closer to those inferred for human populations before the advent of agriculture, with characteristically 20 per cent or more dying before the age of ten years, and fewer than 50 per cent surviving to age fifty. Most of this difference between survivorship curves in developed and developing countries is caused by communicable diseases, ranging from viral and bacterial to protozoan and helminth infections. A more detailed discussion is given by Anderson and May (1991, Chapters 1 and 23.4).

In particular, tuberculosis, which loomed large in Victorian times (carrying off the above-mentioned *Lady of the Camellias*), is often mistakenly thought to be an affliction of the past. On the contrary, tuberculosis remains the world's leading cause of death from any one infectious disease. It currently accounts for an estimated eight million new cases and 2.9 million deaths each year. In the developing world, it is responsible for roughly 7 per cent of all deaths, and 19 per cent of deaths among adults in the age range from fifteen to fifty-nine.

Second, medical complacency about infectious diseases in the developed world is today being shaken by the emergence of seemingly new diseases, and the resurgence of old ones (for example, the incidence of tuberculosis in the USA increased by 18 per cent between 1985 and 1991).

Third, and in many ways most important, the accelerating rate of appearance of resistance to an ever-widening spectrum of antibiotics raises the real possibility that everywhere the hospital wards of the twenty-first century may look more like those of developed countries in the 1930s than those of the 1980s.

Building on these themes, the remainder of this chapter is organized as follows. First, I shall outline an analytic framework, within which the transmission and control of any specific infectious agent may usefully be discussed. Central to this framework is the concept of the 'basic reproductive rate' R_o of the infectious agent. Second, I shall take up the 'changing environments' part of my chapter title to assess how R_o for particular infectious diseases may be affected by changes in population size or social/cultural settings, as well as by changes in the external environment. Here I am clearly interpreting 'changing environments' in a broad sense. Third, I shall briefly venture beyond direct focus on human diseases to sketch how changing environments and changing diseases may affect crops, domestic and wild animals, and even the planet's gene pools of natural products which are, *inter alia*, the sources of new antibiotic drugs. Fourth, I shall amplify my remarks about the widening appearance of resistance to antibiotic agents. I shall conclude by briefly evaluating what I think are major causes for concern as patterns of disease change in response to environmental changes, broadly construed.

THE BASIC REPRODUCTIVE RATE OF AN INFECTIOUS AGENT

The first question that a population biologist asks of any biological population is: what is its basic reproductive rate? How many (female) offspring, on average, is a (female) member of the population intrinsically capable of producing in the absence of 'density-dependent' constraints set by crowding, shortage of food, or other factors? This basic reproductive rate, conventionally denoted by R_o, is not easily assessed, because we rarely see populations free from density-dependent constraints. Nevertheless, R_o remains a key variable characterizing a population's intrinsic dynamics: if R_o exceeds unity, the population is capable of maintaining itself or invading, increasing from small numbers until it is indeed limited by density-dependent factors coming into play; if R_o is less than unity, the population declines from generation to generation and cannot persist.

Medical texts conventionally parcel out infectious diseases according to the taxonomic details of the causative agent: virus, bacteria, protozoa, helminth (parasitic worms). However, for discussion of the transmission—and eventually control—of infection, it makes more sense to focus on the way populations of hosts and infectious agents interact. Anderson and May (1979; 1991, Chapter 2) distinguished two classes of infection: microparasites and macroparasites. Microparasites (which include most viral and bacterial, along with many protozoan, infections) are essentially those where the host population can be partitioned into a few distinct classes: susceptible, infected and infectious, recovered and immune. For macroparasites (which include most helminth and some protozoan infections), in contrast, the pathogenic effects on the host depend on how many worms (or other entities) are present: a light worm burden is of little consequence, and harmful effects are associated with heavy burdens. Therefore mathematical models of macroparasitic infections must deal with the full distribution of parasites among hosts, rather than with the few discrete categories that characterize the mathematically simpler microparasitic infections.

For microparasites, the basic reproductive rate is the number of secondary infections produced, on average, when one infected individual is introduced into a host population where everyone is susceptible. For macroparasites, the definition is somewhat more complicated: it is the number of female offspring produced, on average, throughout the lifetime of a mature female parasite, which themselves achieve reproductive maturity, in the absence of density-dependent constraints. In both cases, R_o is essentially the product of the rate at which an infected individual passes on infection to others, multiplied by the average duration of infectiousness. This duration of infectiousness depends mainly on biological factors intrinsic to the disease in question, and we can usually make a good estimate of it. However, the rate at which new infections are produced is much harder to assess. Indirect methods of assessing the basic reproductive rate for microparasitic infections are surveyed by Anderson and May (1991), who show, for instance, that some typical values of R_o for childhood infections in developed countries are 15–20 for whooping cough, 10–15 for measles, and 5–8 for German measles or poliomyelitis.

In general, the rate at which an infected individual produces new infections will depend on a mixture of biological and social factors. That is, it depends on how many infectious particles are produced, and how many such particles it takes to induce infection, but it also depends on how crowded living conditions are, whether you cover your mouth when you cough, and more generally on standards of hygiene and even nutrition. It follows that this crucial parameter R_o can be affected by changes in population density, changes in social or cultural practices, and changes in the external environment (this is particularly relevant to infections whose transmission involves intermediate vectors such as mosquitoes, flies, or snails). Such changes may even carry R_o from below to above unity or the converse, thus causing a new disease to appear or an old one to disappear. I now turn to survey some past and present examples of this.

CHANGING ENVIRONMENTS AND R_o

Changes in population size and density

As population sizes and densities grow, the number of contacts with other individuals tends to increase. Thus R_o generally increases with population size N, although the relation is rarely directly linear. It follows that the make-or-break point, $R_o = 1$, translates directly into a threshold population size: below this threshold population size, R_o is below unity and the infection cannot be maintained; above the threshold population, R_o exceeds unity and the infection can maintain itself and spread within the population.

For example, estimates suggest that the threshold population for measles is around 300 000 (Bartlett 1957; Black 1966). Similar numbers probably pertain to most of what used to be called childhood infections in developed countries, mainly because the short period of infection (typically around a week or so), coupled with lifetime immunity following recovery, implies that a lot of people are needed to keep the infection ticking over. One implication is that such infections could not persist in earlier hunter–gatherer human societies. Almost certainly, these infections have only been with us since some time after the beginning of the Agricultural Revolution, around 10 000 years ago, when human aggregations began to be large enough to exceed the epidemiologically appropriate threshold sizes.

Broad and basic patterns in human history can be interpreted on this basis (McNeill 1976). At the most general level, the record of human population growth has not been one of steadily accelerating increase but rather is characterized by three distinct phases: hunter–gatherer, agricultural, and the scientific technological phase which began a few hundred years ago. The agricultural phase was characterized by a rapid rise in populations, by a factor of roughly 20, over the first 5000 years, followed by a relative slowing (a further increase by a factor of 5) in the second 5000 years. This slowing very likely resulted from the establishment, and subsequent impact, of microparasitic infectious diseases, such as smallpox, tuberculosis, measles, and so on, as threshold population sizes were exceeded (Anderson and May 1991, Chapter 23). At a more detailed level, current thinking is that the European diseases brought to the New World in the wake of Columbus (and often carried along trade routes in advance of the Europeans themselves) may have reduced indigenous populations in both North and South America by a factor of 10. Certainly such diseases were the biological agents with which Europeans overran the New World. Why did the New World not reciprocate with its own panoply of plagues, novel to Europeans? Almost surely, the answer is because population sizes in the New World were too small, or had become sufficiently large too recently, to maintain such lethal microparasitic infections.

Today, human population numbers continue to grow at rates much greater than anything experienced in our history before the second half of the twentieth century. There is little sign of slowing, and no sign at all in Africa. Many religious leaders encourage such growth among their adherents (seemingly caring about nothing except market share). The world's overall population growth rate of around 2 per cent per year, which represents a doubling every 35 years or so, contains a great deal of variability from region to region, and even from country to country. For some European countries the growth rate is currently around zero, while in some African countries it approaches 4 per cent per year. Iran, for example, has seen its population grow from 29 million to 60 million over the past 14 years, savage wars and internal purges notwithstanding.

Concomitant with such variability in population growth rates are great differences among countries in the proportions in different age groups. In many Third World countries, 45 per cent or more of the population are under the age of fifteen years. Given that, for a variety of reasons, transmission rates for infectious diseases tend to be higher among children than among adults (Anderson and May 1991, Chapter 9), this creates further epidemiological differences between countries with high and low population growth rates.

Alongside population growth, the past century has seen enormous changes in the proportion of people living in cities and large towns rather than in rural settings. By the United Nations definition, the fraction of the world's population classified as 'urban' was around one in seven at the turn of the century; today it is one in two. Two-thirds of these urban dwellers are in developing countries, and this proportion is estimated to rise to 80 per cent by 2025. Population densities are higher in urban settings, and so these changes also carry implications for the easier maintenance and spread of many infections.

Social and cultural factors and R_o

Cutting across the connections I have just made between threshold population sizes and the spread of infection is the fact that, over the past two centuries or so, population sizes in developed countries have increased but the impact of infectious diseases has, on the whole, decreased. Thus, in developed countries, mortality and morbidity from scarlet fever, diphtheria, and other diseases that afflicted the heroines of Victorian novels, together with real Victorians, steadily declined throughout the nineteenth century (McKeown 1979). The advent of antibiotics in the 1930s and 1940s marked a further decline. Later, beginning in the 1960s, vaccination programmes saw an end of many of these infections. However, the declining incidence and impact was a nineteenth century phenomenon, clearly preceding antibiotics or vaccination. This ill-understood phenomenon has been called the 'epidemiological transition'.

Although the 'epidemiological transition' in developed countries is well documented, the causes are disputed. One school attributes the marked decrease in morbidity and mortality from infectious diseases in late Victorian Europe and the USA to a general increase in nutritional standards (McKeown 1979). Others attribute it to higher standards of public and private hygiene (although McKeown is scornful of this, saying that 'washing hands is no more effective than wringing them'). A third possibility lies in the genetics of host populations and of the infection; we could be seeing the results of selection for more resistant hosts, or less virulent strains of infection, or some mixture (these questions are more complex than they might appear: glib views that 'successful parasites evolve to be harmless' fail close analysis, because what is really selected for is reproductive success and if this means being nasty, so be it; see Anderson and May 1991, Chapter 23). Clearly, some form of environmental change underlies the documented epidemiological transition in developed countries, but whether the change involved nutrition, hygiene, genetics, or some mixture is uncertain.

What is certain is that there is no analogy between what may have happened as population grew alongside growing prosperity in nineteenth century Europe and the USA, and what is currently happening as populations burgeon in Third World countries. The epidemiological transition in developed countries in the nineteenth century is a term for a phenomenon that we do not understand, in a social and cultural setting very different from that of most developing countries today.

Three examples of currently emergent or resurgent diseases that are associated with environmental changes are HIV/AIDS, tuberculosis, and Lyme disease.

Molecular studies of the 'phylogeny' or evolutionary history of HIV, the virus which causes AIDS, suggest that it may have diverged from parallel viruses found in monkeys (and that HIV-1 and HIV-2, the two distinct strains afflicting humans, may have diverged from each other) around 1000 years ago. Currently, HIV infects an estimated ten million people, and the real number could be significantly larger. Records are still poor in many places, but the number of people who have gone on to develop AIDS runs from around a third of a million to a million. AIDS is already the leading cause of death among men aged twenty-five to forty in several Central African countries.

From the definition given earlier, the basic reproductive rate of HIV can be written as $R_o = \beta c D$, where D represents the average duration of infectiousness (in years) and βc is the average number of new infections produced (each year) by an infected individual in the early stages in the epidemic, when essentially all partners will be as yet uninfected. In turn, this infection rate is the product of the average probability β of infecting an uninfected partner and the average rate c of acquiring new sexual or needle-sharing partners. Thus defined, R_0 depends on both intrinsic biological and social/cultural factors: D depends on the biology of HIV/AIDS (possibly modified by nutritional state to some extent); β is a mixture of biology and culture (transmission probabilities in unprotected sex are roughly 10 per cent female to male and male to male, and 20 per cent male to female, over the duration of a partnership, but these average odds have high variability and depend only weakly on the actual number of sexual acts; the probabilities are substantially reduced by use of condoms); c, the rate of partner acquisition, clearly depends on behaviour and is subject to great variability within and between groups.

So why did HIV/AIDS emerge so recently, if the virus is a millennium or more old? Of course, it may be that although the virus diverged from other simian immunodeficiency viruses a long time ago, the mutations which made it so lethal to humans only happened very recently. However, it may have been around for some time, episodically appearing and dying out again in rural populations, in cultural settings where social norms kept the average value of partner-change rates c to levels where R_0 was below unity. Thus the global emergence of HIV could have resulted from mutational events which modified the virus in such a way as effectively to increase β (transmission probability) or D (duration of infectiousness), or it could have resulted mainly from cultural changes which raised average values of c (initially among homosexual men in large cities in developed countries, and more generally along truck routes and in large cities in parts of Central Africa), or from some combination of these factors. In any event, the end result is an increase in R_0 to levels significantly in excess of unity.

Lacking an effective drug or vaccine, the only control measures against HIV at present are those which alter behaviour in ways which reduce R_o, ideally to below unity. Such measures may be directed at reducing the transmission parameter β (condoms or sterilizing needles among intravenous drug users), or at reducing the average value of c (reducing numbers of sexual or needle-sharing partners). These are examples of changing the epidemiology of the disease by changing its environment, broadly defined.

I alluded to tuberculosis in my introduction, and particularly to its rising incidence in the USA. Why is this happening? Bloom and Murray (1992) survey a variety of changes in the environmental setting of tuberculosis in the USA which they believe have combined to result in its resurgence. First, the HIV epidemic has enabled tuberculosis to flourish within individuals whose immune system is severely compromised. Second, the increasing number of homeless people in the USA creates a high potential for transmission within a subpopulation whose adverse living conditions result in lower standards of nutrition and hygiene (a reverse epidemiological transition, in effect). Third, many of the growing population of intravenous drug users have adverse living conditions similar to the homeless. Fourth, all these first three factors roil together, reinforcing each other. Fifth, reduced funding has meant that most city and state governments in the USA have been unable to maintain, much less increase, spending on tuberculosis treatment programmes.

Lyme disease is less fearful, and less widespread, than HIV/AIDS or tuberculosis. In its advanced stages, it causes chronic inflammatory arthritis akin to the more familiar rheumatoid arthritis. The disease occurred sporadically in the USA in the nineteenth century, and is occasionally found in the UK today, but it emerged from relative obscurity in the mid-1970s by causing an epidemic of arthritis in the village of Old Lyme in Connecticut. More than 10 000 cases were reported in the USA in 1992. The disease is carried by a deer tick, *Ixodid dammini*, which has become much more common in woodlands in the USA, especially in the northeast, mainly because of explosive growth in deer populations (which in turn derives largely from misplaced sentimentality). In short, Lyme disease is another example of a disease whose greatly enhanced incidence derives from environmental change, basically in the form of unchecked deer populations. Lyme disease responds to prompt treatment with antibiotics, but the real solution here is reduced deer populations.

Changes in the external environment and R_o

Currently, the amount of CO_2 in the atmosphere is increasing by 1–2 per cent each year, mainly as a result of the burning of fossil fuels but also (perhaps 25 per cent of total) from burning tropical forests. At this rate, atmospheric CO_2 will double by the middle of the next century. Computer models for the effects that this will have on average temperatures are still beset by many uncertainties, but the consensus is that a doubling of CO_2 is likely to increase global average temperatures by 1–5 °C.

It is not easy to say what such a temperature increase, especially in the upper range of 5 °C, will mean for biological systems (Dobson *et al.* 1989). Although temperatures were 5 °C lower than they are now at the peak of the last Ice Age, some 10 000 years ago, the last time that they were 5 °C higher was about 20 million years ago. At that time, we were Miocene apes. Such uncertainties are compounded by the fact that geographical ranges of species are set not only by climate boundaries and topographic features, but also to an important degree by interactions with other species. In the words of Vermeij (1991, p. 1100) 'as environments around the world are being disturbed and as species are being exploited and eliminated on an ever increasing scale, this phenomenon of geographical release is likely to become more common'.

Thus impending changes in the global climate are likely to affect the ranges and geographical distribution patterns of many important vectors of disease. These climate changes will be compounded by deforestation, urbanization, and other factors. Interactions among species further cloud any projections.

Looking back to the past, we can see how relatively small environmental changes had large effects on disease. Braudel (1972) emphasizes the many ways in which malaria affected the economic and social history of the Mediterranean World, before changing climate and marshland drainage altered the geographical range of the *Anopheles* mosquito vectors. Rogers and Randolph (1988) have shown how tsetse flies, the vectors of trypanosomiasis (sleeping sickness) among domestic and wild ruminants as well as humans, have influenced patterns of colonization and exploitation in central and western Africa over many centuries. They emphasize how environmental changes, past and present, affect tsetse ranges, with many knock-on effects.

A short list of major diseases whose vector distribution is likely to be affected by climate changes is formidable. Malaria, carried by mosquitoes, heads the list, with problems highlighted by our past failures to control these vectors. In the New World, we have leishmaniasis, carried by a sandfly. In the Old World, we have onchocerciasis or river blindness, a microfilarial infection transmitted by a fly. In both, we have schistosomiasis, whose snail vectors have flourished as unintended side-effects of irrigation schemes. In Asia, dengue haemorrhagic fever is carried by *Aedes* mosquitoes; the incidence of this illness has seen recurring local surges, largely owing to the friendly environment provided for the vector by stagnant water associated with sprawling shanty towns. The epidemiology of most of these diseases is currently changing in various ways, some favourable (as targeted control programmes against the vector of onchocerciasis succeed) and some adverse (as earlier programmes against dipteran vectors break down, and resistance to drugs and insecticides appears). How major geographical range changes, associated with climate change of the magnitude foreshadowed for the middle of the next century, will influence patterns of disease is anyone's guess.

ENVIRONMENTAL CHANGE AND DISEASES OF CROPS AND ANIMALS

The same factors that are likely to affect the geographical distribution of insect and mollusc vectors of human diseases are relevant to many diseases of plants and animals.

Crops and their pathogens and pests

Environmental changes influence the geographical distribution of insects which carry plant diseases or which eat plants. Such changes can also have a direct effect on the susceptibility of plants to attacks by pathogens or pests.

In particular, common atmospheric pollutants such as SO_2 or various oxides of nitrogen (NO_x) can increase the susceptibility of plants to fungal pathogens and to insect herbivores. Any gardener will be interested to learn that aphids are simply not mentioned in early gardening books dating before the high flood of the Industrial Revolution in the nineteenth century (Bell *et al.* 1993). This anecdotal observation is supported by some eighty-three controlled experimental studies, thirty-nine of which found statistically significant correlations between the extent of aphid attack on various plants and the intensity of SO_2 pollution (a further thirty-four found positive correlation, but not significant at the 95 per cent level) (Bell *et al.* 1993). These effects were found in both native vegetation and crops.

Other studies have shown how SO_2 and NO_x pollution can alter the surface chemistry of leaves, rendering the plant more susceptible to fungal infection. These documented associations between pollution and increased incidence of fungal attack are not due to some general 'stress', but to specific mechanisms associated with leaf biochemistry.

Animals and their diseases

Bucke (1993) has made a survey of infectious diseases and cancers of commercially important fish species in the North Sea. There are broad and significant correlations, showing higher prevalence of disease in those areas of the North Sea most affected by pollution. Although the diseases are correlated with environmental disturbance, the causes are not clear. Most researchers believe that 'stress' on the fish in polluted environments results in some loss of immunocompetence, but clear-cut proof is lacking. Furthermore, the data are rather suspect, subject to the bias that they are mainly epiphenomena of fishing activity.

Other instances of disease among marine organisms raise questions as to whether what we are seeing are natural or human-induced events. For example, was the distemper virus that wrought such havoc among seals in the North Sea relatively recently a manifestation of a recurring event (crudely akin to influenza epidemics in humans, although more lethal) or was it amplified, or even caused, by pollution-induced stress? Was the virus that all but eliminated urchins throughout the Caribbean in the 1980s, with consequent alterations in coral communities, a natural manifestation of alternative metastable states, with natural epidemics as the mediator, or was it enhanced, or even created, by human insults? We know too little to answer these questions.

Bovine spongiform encephalitis (BSE or 'mad cow disease') is another ill-understood disease, whose recent origin is fairly clearly tied to a specific change in what could be called the farm environment. It is suspected that BSE was introduced into cattle in the UK by the new practice of 'enriching' commercial foodstuff with sheep offal; in this view, BSE is a transmogrified form of scrapie, the prion infection (akin to Creutzfeldt–Jakob disease or kuru among humans) which has been endemic in domestic sheep populations for as long as anyone can remember. Why people should become so excited about BSE when they have been eating sheep for years is

been more diligent, the table could have been much larger
many other similar entries.

e success of the pharmaceutical industry in creating new
icrobial agents should not be underestimated. Today, the
al that can be drawn upon to combat infectious diseases
rises more than fifty penicillins, seventy cephalosporins,
e tetracyclines, and eight aminoglycosides, along with
bactams, carbapenems, macrolides, streptogramins, di-
folate reductase inhibitors, and others. Neu (1992) pres-
a sweeping survey of the inroads that resistance has made
his arsenal, giving details of seventy-six examples of anti-
s used against specific and significant human infections.
ese examples, twenty-four (32 per cent) are such that
believes that resistance poses a 'crisis now'. For a further
-five (46 per cent), resistance is currently at a level such as
licate 'future crisis'. Overall, for fifty-nine of the seventy-six
ples (78 per cent), resistance has already rendered the
iotic useless against a particular infection, or it will soon.
e very success of antibiotics against infectious diseases has
d with it the seeds of this resistance crisis. Widespread
ive use, and resistance undercutting usefulness, are the
nd yang of evolution. The wider the use, the greater are
elective pressures for resistance. If the composition of our
ital wards is not to return to that of the 1930s, we need
r control of antibiotics (they are consumed like lollipops
me parts of the world, and cattle-feed programmes in
USA are not much better), better hygiene, and more
spread immunization programmes where appropriate (to
ce background incidence of infection), along with a healthy
energetic research base to support the synthesis of agents
improved or novel forms of antimicrobial activity.

CLUSION

ughout history, people have felt their own times to be
al: the best of times, the worst of times, occasionally

another question. BSE stands as a singular case where changing
environmental practices have probably created a new disease in
a domestic animal.

Environmental change, biological diversity, and tomorrow's pharmacology

Each year, 1–2 per cent of the planet's tropical forests are felled,
often irreversibly, and the rate is accelerating. If continued, this
process will see the tropical forests essentially all gone by the
end of the century, just as Britain's original forests disappeared
centuries ago.

With this deforestation goes loss of plant species. A rough
but general (and well-documented) rule states that for every 4
per cent loss of forest area there is likely to be a concomitant
loss of 1 per cent of the species. While this may have much to
do with the psychic health of *Homo sapiens*, what relevance
has it to disease? Most of our antibiotics and other drugs
used against diseases derive ultimately from natural products,
and tomorrow's antibiotics and other drugs are likely to come
from the vast and yet unexplored reservoir of tropical plant
species. Currently, 25 per cent of the drugs on the shelves
in the pharmacy derive from a mere 120 species of plants.
But, throughout the world, the traditional medicines of native
peoples make use of around 25 000 species of plants (about 10
per cent of the total number of plant species).

Clearly, we have much to learn. It seems a pity to be burning
the books before we read them, when their pages potentially
hold tomorrow's pharmaceutical recipes.

EVOLUTION OF RESISTANCE TO ANTIBIOTICS

I opened this chapter by contrasting the patients in a typical
hospital ward in a developed country in the 1930s with the
corresponding patients today. This contrast derives from the

success of antibiotics against infectious diseases, coupled with vaccination programmes.

However, over the past several years an accelerating number of infections have developed resistance to antibiotic drugs, and sometimes to entire spectra of antibiotics. Such resistance is seen most markedly and worryingly in hospital settings, but it is also widespread in the outside community. This rising incidence of antibiotic resistance is causing increased morbidity, mortality, and health care costs.

At the level of anecdote, I note the sense of public disbelief when Jim Henson, the creator of Kermit the Frog, died of what seemed an ordinary streptococcal infection. Such infections have normally been routinely and successfully treated with penicillin. Henson's antibiotic-resistant streptococcal infection proceeded rapidly to fulminating and fatal pneumonia.

The rise in the incidence of tuberculosis in the USA is further complicated by drug-resistant strains. In New York City in 1982 and 1984, 10 per cent of new patients were resistant to one or more drugs; by 1991, this figure had risen to 23 per cent. The resistant proportion among relapsing or previously treated patients was much higher, being 44 per cent in 1991. Incidentally, this points to part of the problem: many tuberculosis patients, especially those with HIV/AIDS, fail to complete their course of drug therapy, which constitutes the ideal environment for selection for resistant strains. Such antibiotic-resistant strains of tuberculosis have adverse implications for both individuals and the community. For individuals infected with multidrug-resistant strains of tuberculosis, the fatality rate is above 50 per cent and is similar to that for untreated cases. For the community, there is a monetary cost: the average costs of treating an antibiotic-susceptible case of tuberculosis is around $12 000, but for a multidrug-resistant case this soars to around $180 000.

A more analytic picture is given in Table 6.1. This table, derived from several sources, conveys a depressing impression of many different infections involving resistance to many different antibiotics, and in many cases at an increasing rate.

Table 6.1 Case studies in resistance

Organism or infection	Antibiotic	Fraction of isolates showing resistance (%) and date (place)
Enterococci	Vancomycin	0.8 1988 (USA)
		4.0 1991 (USA)
Tuberculosis	Isoniazid and rifampin	0.5 1982–4 (USA)
		3.1 1991 (USA)
		19 1992 (NYC)
Shigellosis spp.	Ampicillin	32 1986 (USA)
Shigellosis spp.	Trimethoprinsulphamethoxazole	7 1986 (USA)
Shigella dysenteriae	Resistance to all oral antimicrobial agents in country	100 1991 (Brunei)
Salmonella	Antimicrobial resistance (general)	16 1979 (USA)
		24 1984 (USA)
		32 1989 (USA)
Gonorrhoeae	Penicillin	3 1988 (USA)
		10 1990 (USA)
Gonorrhoeae	Tetracycline	4 1988 (USA)
		6 1990 (USA)
Haemophilus ducreyi	Erythromycin and	

both together. But our own time, coincidentally resonant with the turn of a millennium, is truly significant by any objective measure. Although humans have had major effects on their environment since they first began hunting with fire hundreds of thousands of years ago, it is only very recently that our activities have begun to equal, in scale and scope, the natural processes that built and maintain the biosphere as a place where life can flourish. One single statistic summarizes this: today something like 40 per cent of the global net primary productivity is sequestered for human use (Vitousek *et al*. 1986). Associated with this, the biologically available amounts of key elements such as carbon, nitrogen, sulphur, and phosphorus which circulate in the atmosphere as a result of human activities have risen to be of the same order of magnitude as the amounts cycling from natural processes.

Human activities and impacts on such a scale cause many forms of environmental change. Population growth itself, and associated patterns of urbanization, make it easier for many diseases—particularly directly transmitted microparasitic diseases—to maintain themselves, as host populations move to values well above threshold densities for particular infections. Indeed, population growth is the engine from which all other environmental changes ultimately derive, and the world's population continues to grow at rates which defy intuitive comprehension: 10 000 more people (births minus deaths) each hour; 100 million more each year.

As discussed above, associated destruction of natural habitats, deforestation, and probable large-scale changes in global climate patterns resulting from anthropogenic inputs of greenhouse gases to the atmosphere all imply that epidemiological patterns of disease incidence are likely to change markedly over the next several decades. This is true both for directly and indirectly transmitted human diseases, in both developed and developing countries, and for diseases of domestic and natural plants and animals.

Although all this is true, I end this chapter by emphasizing that the changes in patterns of disease which environmental changes are likely to cause will probably be less significant than the disease-pattern differences that currently exist between what we *could* do and what we *do* do. The epidemiological differences between developed and developing countries today are more pronounced, and more troubling, than any epidemiological differences I expect to see between Western countries today and 50 years from now. Most of the problems discussed in this chapter, having to do with probable changes in disease patterns caused by changing environments, can be remedied or compensated for by appropriate activity. But whether we will in fact implement such remedial or compensatory steps is another question. The remarkable disparities in levels of public health which exist today, within and between countries, do not augur well for our ability to handle future challenges.

When I say that the epidemiological changes likely to result from environmental changes over the next several decades are, to me, less worrying than the present differences in patterns of disease between developed and developing countries, I have one significant reservation. Although essentially all the problems sketched above can be solved by appropriate understanding and action, the evolution of resistance to the present generation of antibiotics ultimately cannot be so solved. I see the currently accelerating appearance of resistance to antimicrobial drugs by more and more infectious diseases to be the greatest threat that looms under the heading of 'changing diseases in changing environments'. Moreover, resistance cannot be escaped. It is evolutionarily inevitable, part of the same Darwinian challenge and response that forged life on earth. But we can slow the evolution of resistance by wise practices, and we can continue to seek new antibiotics, aided by our ever-growing insights into the molecular architecture of microbes and the human immune system. The problem of antibiotic resistance is not conventionally high on the Green Agenda, but it belongs there. I believe that it heads the list in a chapter which seeks to foresee the disease patterns of the future.

REFERENCES

Anderson, R. M. and May, R. M. (1979). Population biology of infectious diseases. Nature, *London*, **280**, 361–67, 455–61.

Anderson, R. M. and May, R. M. (1991). *Infectious diseases of humans: dynamics and control.* Oxford University Press.

Bartlett, M. S. (1957). Measles periodicity and community size. *Journal of the Royal Statistical Society, Series A*, **120**, 48–70.

Bell, J. N. B., McNeil, S., Houlden, G., Brown, V. C., and Mansfield, P. J. (1993). Atmosphere change: its effects on plant pests and diseases. *Parasitology*, **106**, S11–22.

Black, F. L. (1966). Measles endemicity in insular populations: critical community size and its evolutionary implication. *Journal of Theoretical Biology*, **11**, 207–11.

Bloom, B. R. and Murray, C. J. L. (1992). Tuberculosis: commentary on a reemergent killer. Science, **257**, 1055–64.

Braudel, F. (1972). *Mediterranean and the Mediterranean World in the age of Philip the Second* (2 vols.). Collins, London. (Originally published in French in 1949).

Bucke, D. (1993). Aquatic pollution: effects on the health of fish and shellfish. Parasitology, **106**, 25–37.

Cohen, M. L. (1992). Epidemiology of drug resistance: implications for a post-antimicrobial world. *Science*, **257**, 1050–5.

Dobson, A. P., Jolly, A., and Rubenstein, D. (1989). The greenhouse effect and biological diversity. *TREE*, **4**, 64–8.

McKeown, T. (1979). *The role of modern medicine: dream, mirage or nemesis?* Princeton University Press.

McNeill, W. H. (1976). *Plagues and peoples.* Doubleday, New York.

Neu, H. C. (1992). The crisis in antibiotic resistance. *Science*, **257**, 1064–73.

Rogers, D. L. and Randolph, S. E. (1988). Tsetse flies in Africa, bane or boon? *Conservation Biology*, **2**, 57–65.

Vermeij, G. J. (1991). When biotas meet: understanding biota interchange. *Science*, **253**, 1099–104.

Vitousek, P., Ehrlich, P., Ehrlich, A. and Matson, P. (1986). Human appropriation of the products of photosynthesis. *BioScience*, **36**, 368–73.

7

The relative roles of nature and nurture in common disease[1]

David Weatherall

Professor Sir David Weatherall, FRS, qualified at Liverpool University in 1956; after several junior hospital posts, and a period of National Service in Malaya, he spent four years at Johns Hopkins Hospital, Baltimore. He returned to Liverpool in 1965, where he was appointed Professor of Haemotology in 1971. In 1974 Sir David moved to Oxford, where he was Nuffield Professor of Clinical Medicine until 1992. In that year he was appointed Regius Professor of Medicine at Oxford. In 1979 Sir David was made Honorary Director of the Medical Research Council's Molecular Haemotology Unit; in 1989 he established the Institute of Molecular Medicine, of which he is also Honorary Director, at Oxford. His main research interests have been in the application of molecular biology to clinical medicine, particularly the genetic disorders of haemoglobin. Sir David was knighted in 1987, elected to a Fellowship of the Royal Society in 1977, and made a Foreign Associate of the National Academy of Sciences of the USA in 1990. In 1992 he was elected President of the British Association for the Advancement of Science.

As a result of improvements in nutrition, hygiene, housing, and many other environmental factors, and with the advent of immunization and antibiotics, there has been a major decline in infectious disease in rich industrialized countries over the last half century. At the same time there has been a remarkable increase in the life expectancy of their populations and a reduction in infant mortality. These changes have led to a major

---

[1] This essay is based on my Linacre Lecture of the same title, and the 1992 Harveian Oration delivered to the Royal College of Physicians on 22 October 1992.

shift in the pattern of disease such that the important killers, both in middle life and old age, are now vascular disease and cancer. In addition, our increasingly elderly populations suffer from a variety of chronic disorders which reduce their quality of life and cause a major drain on health resources. Although we have become proficient at patching up these disorders, we have made much less progress towards their prevention or cure.

Over the last 20 years epidemiological studies have changed the way in which we think about our current diseases. Previously, it was the custom to bunch vascular disease and cancer together as 'degenerative disorders', intimating that they might be the natural consequence of ageing. However, it is now believed that many of them can be ascribed, at least in part, to environmental factors, suggesting that they might be preventable. This has led to the expectation that a major change in our diets and lifestyles will have a profound effect on the frequency and severity of many of our major killers; most Western societies are now pinning their hopes for improving health and containing the costs of health care on this premise.

This view of the future of health care raises a number of important questions. First, it is not clear to what extent many of our major diseases are environmental in origin and, even if they are, how far we will be successful in controlling the agents or lifestyles that cause them. In particular, we do not know to what extent our response to our new environment is modified by our genetic make-up. We are equally uncertain about the relative roles of the environment and the ageing process itself in generating some of our intractable diseases.

In this chapter, after a brief view of the development of ideas about chemical individuality, I shall try to assess the relative roles of inheritance and environment in the genesis of some of our common diseases. Taking an evolutionary approach to this question, I shall try to assess the extent to which common diseases reflect maladaptation to our new environments and lifestyles. At the same time, I shall examine the potential of recent advances in the basic medical sciences to resolve some of these problems.

ARCHIBALD GARROD AND CHEMICAL INDIVIDUALITY

Although the notion of individual susceptibility or resistance to disease—'disease diathesis'—has been around for many years, it was the English physician Archibald Garrod who, at about the turn of the century, was the first to suggest a rational explanation for this important phenomenon. Garrod, who spent many of his most productive working years as a physician at St Bartholomew's Hospital, London, and later moved to Oxford to succeed William Osler as Regius Professor of Medicine, became interested in biochemistry through an early association and friendship with Frederick Gowland Hopkins. His work on biochemical individuality was first stimulated by his observations on patients with alkaptonuria. He published his first descriptions of the occurrence of this disease in siblings in 1899 and 1901, the second of which emphasizes the frequency of consanguinity in their parents. Although he did not appreciate the genetic significance of these findings, his paper was seen by William Bateson, the leading protagonist of Mendel's work at the time, who, a month after it appeared, reported Garrod's observations to the Evolution Committee of the Royal Society, recognizing that they suggested a recessive form of inheritance for alkaptonuria.

Garrod continued to study rare biochemical disorders, and in June 1908 delivered the Croonian Lectures to the Royal College of Physicians, entitled 'inborn errors of metabolism'. The lectures were published under the same title as a monograph in 1909 (Garrod 1909). By then Garrod had extended his work on alkaptonuria and had added cystinuria, pentosuria, and albinism to the list of inborn errors. He realized that the homogentisic acid in the urine of alkaptonurics is a normal intermediate in the breakdown of phenylalanine and tyrosine, and concluded that the failure of its further degradation in alkaptonuria must result from the absence of the enzyme required to cleave its benzene ring.

In the introductory chapter to *Inborn errors of metabolism*, quoting Bateson's interpretation of his work, Garrod makes a strong case for the recessive inheritance of these rare diseases. He goes on to develop the idea that they are due to a block in metabolic pathways and that they may well be the tip of the iceberg of biochemical individuality. He ends his introduction as follows (Garrod 1909): 'but each one of them presents peculiar features of much interest which amply repay detailed consideration, if only on account of the light which their study throws upon the chemical processes at work in the normal human organism'.

Over the next few years Garrod continued to think about biochemical individuality and its evolutionary basis. In May 1923 he delivered the Linacre Lecture at Cambridge, entitled 'Glimpses of the higher medicine', in which he discussed the role of science in clinical medicine and the broader biological implications of biochemical individuality (Garrod 1923). He developed the theme that individual variability in response to disease reflects biochemical diversity which must, in turn, be related to evolutionary adaptation. These ideas were summarized in his second book, *Inborn factors in disease*, published in 1931 (Garrod 1931).

Inborn factors is in many ways even more remarkable than *Inborn errors*. It starts with a prologue which reviews the history of the doctrines of diathesis. In the first part he summarizes his ideas about the chemical basis of individuality, the possible role of evolution in modifying disease susceptibility, and the inheritance of what he calls 'morbid liabilities'. In the second part he speculates on how common diseases might be modified by differences in individual susceptibility. He rounds up his thoughts in a brief epilogue which ends with these words (Garrod 1931):

It might be claimed that what used to be spoken of as a diathesis is nothing else but chemical individuality. But to our chemical individualities are due our chemical *merits* as well as our chemical shortcomings; and it is more nearly true to say that the factors which confer upon us our predispositions to, and immunities from the various mishaps which are spoken of as diseases, are inherent in our very chemical structure; and even in the molecular groupings which confer upon us our individualities, and which went to the making of the chromosomes from which we sprang'.

Garrod's remarkable insights went largely unnoticed. When *Inborn factors* was first published it received lukewarm reviews in several journals, none of which suggested that the reviewers had the slightest inkling of the book's message. When Charles Scriver and Barton Childs asked the Delegates of Oxford University Press to reprint it in 1989 their response was lukewarm, although they reluctantly agreed (Scriver and Childs 1989). In the event, it has made little impact on the medical world, and to my knowledge has attracted no reviews.

PROGRESS IN UNDERSTANDING HUMAN GENETICS AND EVOLUTION SINCE GARROD'S TIME

Garrod worked at the beginning of the period which is sometimes called 'classical genetics'. In 1911, three years after his Croonian Lectures, Wilhelm Johannsen published a paper entitled 'The genotype conception of heredity' and used the word 'gene' for the first time (Johannsen 1911). Over the next 50 years enormous progress was made (Bowter 1989). The chromosome theory of inheritance was refined, genetic linkage and chromosome mapping were developed by Morgan and his colleagues, Muller elucidated the mechanisms of mutation, and the work of biometricians, notably Fisher and Haldane, in which statistical techniques were applied to the genetics of large populations, paved the way for the amalgamation of Mendelism and Darwinism which formed the basis of modern evolutionary theory. Progress was equally rapid in biochemical genetics, and, following their classical work on induced mutations in *Neurospora crassa*, Beadle and Tatum were able to enunciate the 'one gene – one enzyme' concept (Beadle 1964):

all biochemical processes in all organisms are under genetic control; these biochemical processes are resolvable into a series of individual stepwise reactions; each biochemical reaction is under the ultimate control of a different single gene; and mutation of a single gene results only in an alteration in the ability of the cell to carry out a single primary chemical reaction.

These remarkable developments in biology coincided with a revolution in physics which had also started in the second half of the nineteenth century and which led to an understanding of atoms and subatomic particles. This, in turn, spawned quantum chemistry which described how atoms bond together to form molecules, and ultimately how large molecules such as proteins are assembled and function. In 1943 Erwin Schrödinger, in his lectures 'What is life', presented a completely new perspective of living things based on the laws of physics. Ultimately, this was to attract physicists and chemists to biology, a movement which culminated in a new discipline—molecular biology.

In the 1940s, a beautifully executed series of experiments by Avery, MacLeod, and McCarty demonstrated that DNA is the informational molecule (Avery *et al.* 1944), and the way in which it plays this role was established in 1953 when Watson and Crick described its structure (Watson and Crick 1953). Within a few years the genetic code had been broken and found to be universal throughout all living organisms, an observation of seminal importance for modern evolutionary theory. A gene could now be defined as a length of nucleotide bases which codes for a particular peptide chain. With the advent of recombinant DNA, it became possible to isolate and sequence genes and to start to determine how they are regulated.

Medical genetics came into its own after the Second World War, first using the techniques of classical genetics, then biochemical genetics, and finally molecular genetics. Enormous progress has been made in determining the molecular basis of single-gene disorders. By the application of genetic linkage studies to isolate genes for different diseases and the use of positional cloning, in which the structure of a gene product is deduced from its DNA sequence, it has been possible to describe the molecular pathology of many diseases for which the cause was unknown up to a few years ago. The sixth edition of *The metabolic basis of inherited disease*, the work that catalogues the inborn errors of metabolism, runs to two enormous volumes, 122 chapters, and over 200 authors (Scriver *et al.* 1989).

Clearly, Garrod's concept of the inborn errors of metabolism has turned out to be remarkably accurate. As he anticipated, not only has this provided valuable information about the biochemistry of human disease, but it has also clarified many normal biological mechanisms. For example, work on the inherited disorders of haemoglobin has yielded valuable information about gene regulation, structure–function relationships in proteins, human evolution, and, as we shall see later, the way in which mutations have become distributed among the populations of the world. But what of his broader views of disease susceptibility when placed in the context of modern evolutionary theory?

There have been major advances in our understanding of human evolution since Garrod's time (Lewin 1989). The mechanisms of mutation, recombination, and other forms of gene shuffling have been identifed as the basis for the alterations in our genetic make-up on which Darwinian selection can work. Since our evolutionary history is written in our proteins and DNA, it is possible to make detailed comparisons of their structures in different groups of organisms and, by estimating the rates of mutation, to start to define the patterns of evolution. As a general approach to taxonomic analysis, we can now determine the relatedness of different species by DNA–DNA hybridization; mismatching due to evolutionary divergence reduces the binding strength between the two DNA molecules. This technique has been used extensively to measure genetic differences between taxonomic groups.

The discovery of restriction fragment length polymorphisms (RFLPs), i.e. harmless alterations in the structure of DNA which are identified by bacterial restriction enzymes, has turned out to be another valuable tool for studying population genetics

and evolution. These harmless polymorphisms are often distributed in blocks, or haplotypes. It turns out that RFLP haplotypes
associated with different gene families, the human globin genes
for example, are quite ancient and thus reflect the way in which
populations have arisen and diverged during human evolution.
Furthermore, in effect we have two evolutionary time clocks
in our genomes, for as well as nuclear DNA there is also
cytoplasmic DNA which encodes for mitochondrial proteins
and enzymes. The mutation rate of mitochondrial DNA is
faster than that of nuclear DNA and, particularly since it is
all inherited from our mothers and therefore is haploid, it is
of great value for population and evolutionary studies.

As well as determining our relatedness to our nearest evolutionary neighbours, studies of mitochondrial and nuclear DNA
polymorphisms have started to yield new information about the
origins of human beings. The study of evolution at the molecular
level helps us to follow their migrations and, when combined
with linguistics and palaeontology, to trace the origins and movements of the different races. Armed with this knowledge, we can
start to ask questions about the mechanisms of the distribution
of genes in populations and how our past environments may
have modified our present genetic constitution.

What, in the light of these remarkable advances, is the current
standing of Garrod's ideas on individual biochemical diversity in
relationship to susceptibility or resistance to common disease?
Although this topic is almost as neglected as it was in Garrod's
time, there are hints that it may be of considerable importance
as we try to understand the causes of the major non-infectious
killers of Western society, and to develop our ideas about their
prevention and management.

DISEASE SUSCEPTIBILITY OR RESISTANCE AS A REFLECTION OF OUR EVOLUTIONARY PAST

In considering the effects of natural selection on our current
genetic make-up it is important to appreciate the time-scale

involved (Lewin 1989). We spent over a million years wandering around in nomadic bands of hunter–gatherers. Agriculture and the formation of settled villages started about 10 000 years ago, and towns and irrigated agriculture have been in existence for about 5000 years. We have only been exposed to our current high technology environments and lifestyles for 150 years. During each of these periods in our evolution we have been exposed to completely different environmental hazards. The low life expectancy of the hunter–gatherers may have been partly the result of infectious disease, but such evidence as there is suggests that accidental and traumatic death, animal predators, infanticide, cannibalism, and warfare may also have been important contributors. The growth of agriculture and increased population density probably saw the emergence of many of the infectious and parasitic killers which are still with us today. Once we became huddled together in insanitary and overcrowded towns, conditions were rife for the major epidemics of infectious disease which devastated entire populations. During the whole of this time the numerous hazards which killed before reproductive age must have led to the selection of a variety of traits which are ill adapted to the completely different environments in which we live today.

It is now clear that as part of the price that we have had to pay for our evolutionary success, we have been left with a spectrum of genetic variability ranging from a high frequency of single-gene disorders to a complex pattern of individual susceptibility in response to common environmental killers.

Single-gene disorders and natural selection

The inherited disorders of haemoglobin, sickle-cell anaemia, and thalassaemia are the commonest single-gene diseases in humans (Weatherall 1991). The World Health Organization has estimated that, by the year 2000, approximately 7 per cent of the world's population will be carriers; if the recent suggestion that the world population will double by the early part of the twenty-first century is correct, and if over 90 per cent of this expansion is confined to the developing world where these diseases are so common, this may be a considerable underestimate. However, if these diseases kill before the age of reproduction, why are they so common? Surely they should have been eliminated by selection. The geneticist J. B. S. Haldane first offered an answer to this conundrum in 1949 (Haldane 1949). He reasoned that, since they are recessive diseases, they might have flourished because heterozygotes are (or were) protected against a major environmental hazard. Since the world distribution of thalassaemia mirrors that of malaria, Haldane made the remarkably astute suggestion that malaria might be the selective agent. More recently, this hypothesis has been extended to cover other common structural variants of haemoglobin, i.e. sickle-cell haemoglobin and haemoglobins C and E.

Although work in Africa over 40 years ago suggested that the sickle-cell trait protects against malaria, until recently it has been very difficult to obtain evidence in support of Haldane's hypothesis, particularly in the case of thalassaemia. Population studies of this type are bedevilled by many problems, including lack of homogeneity, founder effects, and genetic drift. However, with the advent of DNA technology, which allows us to identify individual mutations and to study batteries of neutral DNA polymorphisms, it is now possible to tackle these problems.

There are two major forms of thalassaemia, the α and β types. Over 120 different mutations have been found in patients with β-thalassaemia, and α-thalassaemia is almost as heterogeneous (Weatherall 1991). It is now clear that each population in which these diseases occur at a high frequency have their own particular mutations which, presumably, have been expanded by selection against a locally acting environmental factor. Population studies in Polynesia and Melanesia have shown that malaria has been the major factor in maintaining the high frequency of α-thalassaemia (Hill 1992; Flint *et al.* 1993). Analysis of RFLP haplotypes related to the sickle-cell mutation suggests that it arose more than once during evolution, and recent work in The Gambia suggests that the sickle-cell trait confers approximately 90 per cent resistance against severe forms of *Plasmodium falciparum* malaria (Hill 1992). There is also evidence that the high frequency of haemoglobin E, which is found in millions of carriers in the eastern parts of India, Burma, and throughout Southeast Asia, also results from selection by malaria. Preliminary studies suggest that the protection of heterozygotes for these conditions may be mediated through the ability of their red cells to express either malarial or altered self-antigens more effectively, a mechanism that might speed the removal of parasitized red cells from the circulation (Luzzi *et al*. 1991).

However, globin variants are not the only proteins that have come under intense selection by malaria. Approximately 100 million people are deficient in the red-cell enzyme glucose-6-phosphate dehydrogenase (G6PD) (Hill 1992). Again, it turns out that the molecular basis for G6PD deficiency is extremely heterogeneous and that this widespread enzyme deficiency results from selection by malaria. In parts of Southeast Asia and Melanesia a high proportion of the population have oval red cells. These particular ovalocytes are resistant to invasion by both *P. falciparum* and *Plasmodium vivax*. It has been found recently that this disorder results from a 9-amino acid deletion at the junction of the cytoplasm and membrane-spanning regions of the band C protein of the red-cell membrane (Tanner 1993). Here, therefore, is another mutation which has arisen locally and come under intense selection by malaria; it is quite likely that the homozygous state is lethal.

Blood group antigens have also been called into service in an effort to survive malarial infection. For example, the Duffy antigen is present in the red cells of many populations but is absent in certain parts of Africa (Hill 1992). This particular blood group is involved in the mechanism whereby malaria parasites which cause milder forms of malaria gain entry into red blood cells; blood group O may also be protective against malaria.

However, genetic variability caused by selection against severe malaria does not stop at the red cell. Recent studies in The Gambia have shown that the HLA class I antigen HLA-Bw53 confers 40 per cent protection against both cerebral malaria and severe malarial anaemia, and that the HLA class II antigen HLA-drb1*1302 is strongly associated with protection from severe malarial anaemia (Hill 1992). These findings imply an important role for a limited set of immune responses, involving both HLA class I and class II restricted T lymphocytes, in providing immunity to severe malaria. The major function of HLA molecules is to present short peptides derived from foreign antigens to T lymphocytes; individual HLA types bind and present peptides with different sequences. Thus these new studies offer the possibility of identifying particular malaria antigens which might be good candidates for vaccines.

Therefore it appears that, during the relatively short period that man has been exposed to malaria, natural selection has worked on many genes to mediate protection. The current frequencies of these different polymorphisms vary depending on the degree of protection, the clinical severity of the homozygous state, and many other factors. Many of them are examples of balanced polymorphisms, i.e. their frequency reflects a balance between the early deaths of homozygotes and the relative fitness of heterozygotes. In the case of some of the milder forms of α-thalassaemia, the commonest genetic diseases in humans, there is evidence that the mild homozygotes have come under selection. Thus they may represent transient rather than balanced polymorphisms. In the case of the major haemoglobin disorders and G6PD deficiency, we have been left with a number of extremely common monogenic diseases.

The elegant story of the maintenance of the red-cell and HLA-DR polymorphisms by malaria is a remarkable ratifica-tion of Garrod's thoughts about how biochemical individuality, working through evolution, may alter the pattern of disease. However, it is only the tip of the iceberg. There is little doubt that the infections to which we have been exposed in our evolutionary past have left us with a great deal more genetic heterogeneity, some of which will have major implications for variability in susceptibility or resistance to disease (Weatherall *et al.* 1988) (Table 7.1). For example, it is likely that the distribution of the human blood groups reflects this type of process. Recently it has been suggested that the high frequency of Tay–Sachs disease in certain Jewish populations results from heterozygote resistance to tuberculosis in some of the ghettos of eastern Europe (O'Brien 1991). There is increasing evidence that variability in the HLA-DR system is related to susceptibility to many infectious diseases, including AIDS, and mouse geneticists have been able to define a number of different genes whose mutations confer resistance or susceptibility to bacterial or parasitic illnesses (Weatherall *et al.* 1988).

When we consider the extreme conditions of climatic change and availability of food to which our ancestors were exposed, not to mention their completely different lifestyles, it is unlikely that our biochemical individuality is based solely on selection by infection. The metabolic adaptations which were required during our long period as hunter–gatherers must be very much part of our current genetic make-up.

What other penalties might we be paying for our evolutionary successes in the past?

Genetic constitutions that protected us against epidemics of infectious illnesses or other environmental hazards in the past

Table 7.1 Genetic variability in response to infection

Polymorphisms	
Blood groups	Plague?, Syphilis
Secretor status	Bacterial meningitis, urinary tract infection
HLA-DR	Leprosy, Hepatitis B, AIDS
Monogenic diseases	
Red cell	Malaria
Tay–Sachs	Tuberculosis
Cystic fibrosis	?

may not be suited to the quite different conditions of today. Is it possible that some of the traits that were selected make us more or less likely to develop the common diseases of Western society? The first intimation that this might be so came from observations of the distribution of blood groups and secretor status in patients with common diseases such as peptic ulcer or cancer of the stomach (Mourant *et al.* 1978). Those with blood group A have a greater likelihood of developing gastric cancer than those with group O, who in turn are more prone to duodenal ulcer. More recently the finding of a strong association of certain autoimmune diseases with particular HLA-DR polymorphisms has pointed in the same direction, i.e. that particular adaptations that may have been made in response to infection in the past may not be suited to our current environment.

Much of the evidence that our current killers are the result of our cosy Western environments and bad habits is based on the observation that their prevalence increases in emigrants from countries in which they are less common after they adopt their new lifestyles. However, there are some major inconsistencies. In particular, it is apparent that the response of different populations to 'Westernization' varies considerably, suggesting that genetic factors play an important role in modifying the effects of environmental insults. This is exemplified by the constellation of disorders which anthropologists call the 'New World syndrome'.

The first Americans originated in Asia and gained access to America across the Bering Strait, which separates Alaska from Siberia, about 10 000–15 000 years ago. While the pattern and precise timing of the migration is still disputed, it is clear that these travellers populated both north and south America. By the time Columbus arrived, over a thousand different languages were spoken among the native Indian peoples. The linguist Joseph Greenberg has analysed the 600 languages that have survived and, remarkably, has traced them back to just three roots, findings which are compatible with lineages which have been identified quite recently by mitochondrial DNA studies

(Rogers *et al*. 1992). Over the last few hundred years the Amerindian descendants of the early settlers have been exposed to conditions created by Western industrialization, yet their pattern of diseases is quite different from that of the European settlers with whom they have shared their new environment.

The New World syndrome is characterized by a very high prevalence of obesity at an early adult age, insulin-resistant diabetes, and gallstones and gall-bladder cancer, especially in females (Weiss *et al*. 1984). It appears that this syndrome began, or at least increased dramatically, after the Second World War. The anthropologists who have identified it suggest that it reflects a high frequency of genes that cause susceptibility to environmental agents associated with 'Westernization', and that exist by virtue of selective advantage during or before the initial peopling of the Americas.

The distribution and frequency of the diseases which make up the New World syndrome are so unusual as to leave little doubt that genetic factors are involved. For example, the population of Pima, Arizona, have a nineteen-fold greater incidence of insulin-resistant diabetes than Caucasian populations in other parts of the Americas; an increased frequency has been found in almost all American aboriginals with the exception of Eskimos. It does not matter from which particular tribes they have arisen or where they live, suggesting that the environment is insufficient to explain the high frequency of the disease. As judged by pictorial records, it appears that obesity in young adult Amerindians has become particularly common over the last 50 years. In Pima the prevalence of gallstones in women reaches almost 90 per cent by the age of 65 years. There is a strong relationship between the high frequency of gallstones and the acquisition of gall-bladder cancer. In contrast, the rate of increase of 'Western' tumours in the Amerindian population has been slower than might have been expected. Similarly, the prevalence of heart disease is lagging behind that of diabetes and obesity, again suggesting that the response to a Western environment is different in Amerindian peoples, presumably because of their genetic make-up.

A similar picture has emerged over recent years in some of the island populations of Micronesia and Polynesia (Zimmet *et al*. 1990). Insulin-resistant diabetes and obesity are extremely common in these populations, although their distribution is patchy. For example, there is a very high prevalence of diabetes on Nauru Island; over 60 per cent of the adult population are affected. Nauru is a remote atoll with a population of about 5000 Micronesians. A series of colonizations by British, Australians, and New Zealanders, together with a rapid increase in income from phosphate mining, has completely changed the lifestyle of Naurians. Nearly all their food is now imported and they live on a typical high energy Westernized diet. As well as diabetes, there is a high frequency of obesity which was almost non-existent some years ago and which started to reach epidemic proportions in the 1950s.

The pattern of a dramatic increase in the frequency of obesity and insulin-resistant diabetes is now being seen in many Asian emigrant populations, and is also affecting Australian Aborigines and the Chinese of Singapore (Smith 1992; McKeigue *et al*. 1989), Taiwan, and Hong Kong, although not, so far, the population of mainland China (Table 7.2). There is no doubt that we are seeing the start of a world epidemic of these diseases.

Some years ago, when it started to become apparent that there was a dramatic increase in the prevalence of diabetes in contemporary human populations, one of the founding fathers of human population genetics, James Neel, suggested that it might be due to dietary plenty imposed on what he called a

Table 7.2 Prevalence of insulin-resistant diabetes

North Europeans	2%–4%
American Blacks	4%–6%
South Asians (London)	22%
South Asians (Durban)	22%
Australian Aborigines	20%
Amerindians	10%–80%
Micronesians Polynesians	5%–60%

'thrifty' genotype which had been selected to take advantage of sporadic food availability in primitive societies (Neel 1962). This notion has been extended by Kenneth Weiss and his colleagues (Weiss *et al.* 1984). They suggest that the gene or genes related to food storage in the form of fat may have been particularly advantageous in allowing women to become fertile or to nurse infants in times of Arctic unpredictability, certainly the state which existed when the early settlers of North America crossed the Bering Strait and made their way through the ice-bound American continent. A fat-storage or thrifty metabolic genotype could have had a selective advantage and might explain the New World syndrome and the rapid increase in diseases which result from overexposure to today's excessive diet. Similarly, the founding Nauruans reached their island after long voyages in canoes, which would have made death by starvation a high probability.

The pattern that is emerging is that many races of Asian origin seem to have a genetic propensity to obesity and insulin-resistant diabetes. However, there is increasing evidence that this may also be the case for some populations of African origin. Therefore it is possible that at least some facets of the thrifty genotype reflect very ancient genetic polymorphisms. If so, why do they not occur at higher frequencies in European populations? Of course, it could be that those who populated Europe did not undergo such selective privations. Alternatively, it is possible that in some environments their deleterious effects may have been relatively greater over a longer period; in Nauru, insulin-resistant diabetes affects many individuals of reproductive age. However, whatever the explanation, it seems inescapable that what we are seeing in Nauru and Pima, and in many other populations, is the effect of Westernization on a genotype which is ill adapted to its new environment—an extreme example of the pattern of illness that may be affecting most developed countries.

Twin and family studies suggest that insulin-resistant diabetes has a strong genetic component. Recent work on families in which this condition occurs early in life and follows a dominant inheritance suggests that in some, but not all, cases the condition is linked to the locus for the enzyme glucokinase on chromosome 7 (Spielman and Nussbaum 1992; Frougel *et al.* 1993). Even more remarkably, in some of these families structural studies of the glucokinase gene have shown mutations that would, in effect, inactivate it. At the time of writing over twenty different mutations of this gene have been identified. Since glucokinase is a key enzyme in mediating the insulin response to glucose, it is a good candidate to be a major player in the genesis of insulin-resistant diabetes. Interestingly, a recent study of Africans has shown a modest association between a particular pattern of RFLPs related to the glucokinase gene and the likelihood of developing this form of diabetes (Chui *et al.* 1992).

It is already clear, however, that many other genes will be involved in type 2 diabetes (Groop *et al.* 1993; Leahy and Boyd 1993). In some families, linkage has been established to a so far unidentified gene on the long arm of chromosome 20. In others there appears to be an important gene on chromosome 19, and quite recently this has been identified as that coding for another important enzyme in glucose metabolism, glycogen synthase. A few families have been found with extreme insulin resistance due to mutations of the insulin receptor gene or structural abnormalities of insulin itself.

However, it is already clear that none of these mutations is likely to be the major cause of the forms of insulin-resistant diabetes that are so common in many populations. It is clear from our discussion of malaria that a wide range of genetic modifications will be generated by natural selection in an attempt to protect against serious environmental hazards. In evolutionary terms, we have only been exposed to malaria for a short time, perhaps a few thousand years. The thrifty genotype may reflect a much older series of adaptations. Thus, encouraging as this work is, we may only be scratching the surface of its complexities. We shall have to learn much more about the genetics of energy metabolism and obesity before we start to understand this intriguing constellation of disorders.

What of other polygenic diseases? It seems likely that the same principles will be involved. Genotypes which were selected during our period as hunter–gatherers and which have helped us combat hazards in the past are unlikely to be suited to our current environment. A blood coagulation system which may have been effective in the bush may be quite inappropriate for our sedentary lives of today. Similarly, the chemical pathways which evolved to regulate salt and water or cholesterol metabolism during periods of extreme environmental conditions may be completely at variance with our salt-rich high energy Western diets.

Research into the genetic influences that make us more or less prone to coronary artery disease exemplifies the complexity of studying polygenic disorders. To start with, information gleaned from twin studies suggests that this will not be an easy problem; with a concordance rate of only 20–30 per cent for coronary artery disease in identical twins, it is clear that our genes play only a modest role in the cause of this disease and that our environment is of particular importance. Much recent work has concentrated on trying to determine the genetic regulation of the levels of blood cholesterol and other clotting factors of major importance in the genesis of vascular disease.

Cholesterol is an important component of cell membranes. However, the very property that makes it useful in this respect, i.e. its complete insolubility in water, makes it lethal in the wrong place, such as the walls of arteries. Hence it has to be transported in a safe state in the blood and, to this end, is packaged in the cores of carrier molecules called plasma lipoproteins. Much of our cholesterol is carried in the so-called 'low density lipoproteins' (LDLs). Brown and Goldstein (1988) have shown that blood cholesterol levels are modified by the activity of specific receptors which bind LDLs optimally at cholesterol concentrations of 2.5 mg/dl. These authors have calculated that a blood level of 25 mg/dl, i.e. about one-fifth of the level usually seen in Western societies, would be sufficient to nourish all our body cells with cholesterol.

The level of cholesterol is under complex genetic control.

From the work of Brown and Goldstein it is now known that over 150 different mutations of the LDL receptor occur, many of which give rise to a condition called monogenic hypercholesterolaemia (Hobbs *et al.* 1992). The carrier state for this disorder, which is associated with a high frequency of coronary artery disease, occurs in about 1 in 500 of the population.

There is a large family of carrier proteins for cholesterol. One which has been particularly well characterized is apolipoprotein B-100. It turns out that as many as 1 in 500 subjects in Europe and North America are carriers for a particular mutation of the gene for this protein, which causes a marked elevation in the level of cholesterol in their blood and a propensity for premature coronary artery disease (Tybjaerg-Hansen and Humphries 1992). The gene for another carrier protein of this type, apolipoprotein E, has also been found to be the site of mutations which, though rare, are associated with increased levels of lipid. Similarly, mutations of other genes involved in lipid metabolism may have the same effect. There is increasing evidence that genetic polymorphisms of the different genes involved in lipid transport are related to susceptibility to coronary artery disease.

Studies of some of our key blood clotting factors are also starting to unravel part of the genetic basis for vascular disease. Epidemiological work has suggested that the level of fibrinogen in our blood is of major importance in determining the likelihood of a heart attack (Humphries *et al.* 1992). Some progress has been made in defining the changes in the fibrinogen gene which results in more effective formation of its product.

Very recently, it has been found that variability of a gene which is responsible for the production of a protein called angiotensin-converting enzyme (ACE) may be another major player in determining susceptibility to heart disease (Bell 1992). The primary action of ACE is to convert a protein called angiotensin 1 to angiotensin 2, a potent constrictor of blood vessels. However, it may also play a role in degrading several other potent agents which are involved in regulating the size of our blood vessels. Preliminary studies suggest that individuals with a particular variation of their ACE genes are more likely to develop heart attacks. Even more importantly, this work suggests that genetic variability involving the production of ACE may account for up to 30 per cent of heart attacks in individuals who have no other risk factors, i.e. they do not smoke and they have low blood cholesterol levels and other features which would make them less likely to have coronary artery disease.

There has also been considerable progress towards identifying some of the genes involved in autoimmune diseases like type 1 diabetes and multiple sclerosis. Here, polymorphisms of the HLA-DR gene family seem to be particularly important, but it is quite clear from work in both humans and mice that many other genes may be involved, particularly in the case of type 1 diabetes. Progress has also been made in tackling the genetics of other common diseases including allergy and atopy, early onset Alzheimer's disease, and several chronic skin disorders. It seems very likely that over the next few years we shall start to define at least some of the major gene loci involved in making us more or less susceptible to our common killers and degenerative disorders. We shall then have the daunting task of putting all this information together to understand how these complex genetic interactions combine with many different environmental factors to generate these diseases.

LESSONS FOR THE FUTURE

Thoughtful critics of modern medical practice like Thomas McKeown and others are concerned about our current obsession with disease mechanisms and our disregard for the prevention of disease by controlling the environmental factors which, they believe, are at the root of most of them (McKeown 1988). McKeown's view is that, apart from monogenic diseases and congenital malformations, the bulk of the major killers in Western society are due entirely to our unfriendly environment and to our diets and lifestyles, and that medical education and practice should change from the study of intrinsic disease and its management to concentrating on epidemiology, preventative medicine, and public health.

Over the last few years this approach to medical care has become extremely popular and the centrepiece of Government health care programmes. There is a growing cynicism about the value of the basic medical sciences for day-to-day clinical practice, an attitude which is being encouraged by the bad press being received by modern science as a whole.

No one can deny that during the short time that we have been exposed to our increasingly artificial industrial environment there has been no time for us to alter our genetic make-up, which is still adapted to the life of a hunter–gatherer. Therefore should we, as suggested by McKeown and others, forget about our genes and simply carry on with trying to modify our lifestyles and environment? However, since we do not yet know the degree to which we are ill adapted to our modern environment, it is difficult to predict how far we will be able to control our current killers by modifying it. This problem is accentuated by our increasing ability to change our environment over short periods of time. In addition, for many diseases we have no idea about the relative role of the environment and endogenous factors.

These uncertainties about the environmental causes of disease and our ability to control them are exemplified by our current knowledge of the biology of cancer. Recent work suggests that neoplastic transformation results from the acquisition of a critical number of mutations in cellular oncogenes, i.e. genes that are involved in the regulation of cellular growth, proliferation, and differentiation. We may be born with these mutations, but more commonly they result from environmental carcinogens or endogenous damage to our DNA. While cigarette smoke is the major carcinogen in the generation of lung cancer, the evidence for the role of diet and other aspects of our lifestyle or environment as the cause of cancer is less certain (Doll and Peto 1981). Furthermore, as pointed out by Ames and his colleagues, malignant disease is an age-related phenomenon in most species (Ames 1988). It may be accelerated by exposure to environmental carcinogens, but it also reflects endogenous oxidant production and damage to DNA. The short answer is that, with some notable exceptions, we are uncertain about the extent to which the environment is responsible for cancer, and even if it turns out that it is, how far we can modify it. For many other diseases of Western society—diabetes, arthritis, the major psychoses, dementia, and the rest—the relative role of nature and nurture is even less clear.

It is likely that, because of adaptations made in our evolutionary past, we are ill equipped for life in our high energy, industrialized Western societies. As the developing world changes its lifestyle the same problems will arise and, as we have seen in the case of Amerindians and Asians, they may be exaggerated. If the whole of mankind has cholesterol levels that are too high (Chen *et al*. 1991), it seems unlikely that we will ever be able to control vascular disease completely by alterations in our diet or lifestyle. Similarly, although we may make inroads into the reduction in the death rates due to cancer, it seems likely that this disease will always be with us. When it comes to our other major killers we have no way of controlling them by modification of our environment because we have no idea what causes them.

Of course we should do what we can towards reducing the frequency of our major killers where there is solid evidence about the action of particular environmental factors, but we would be unwise to put all our eggs in the environmental basket. The definition of the major genes involved in susceptibility or resistance to our common killers, particularly when studied in their evolutionary context, offers us an extremely valuable approach to determining the basic mechanisms involved in their generation. If, for example, we could define the important genes involved in susceptibility to heart disease and compare their products with those of the same genes that are not associated with susceptibility, we might well start to understand the underlying cause of coronary artery disease and hence how best to treat it. Of course, it is also possible that by approaching our common diseases in this way, we might learn how to define a subset of individuals on whom we should concentrate our efforts in preventive medicine.

It is essential that we maintain a two-pronged attack, doing what we can to prevent our common diseases by modification of our environment and lifestyle, but at the same time encouraging basic research into their cause using the extremely valuable new tools that are now available to us. Like the work of Garrod, it may be many years before the fruits of our current basic medical research, using the tools of the 'new biology', are seen in the clinic. But it is quite clear from the remarkable insights that Garrod left behind, that this is the only way forward, a message which we have to impress upon our governments, medical educationalists, and those who support medical research.

SUMMARY

The current intractable diseases of industrialized countries, which will also affect the developing world as it becomes richer, reflects the effects of environment, genetic constitution, and pathology which may be an inevitable consequence of ageing. Hence, although much can be done to combat some of our major killers, we would be unwise to depend entirely on the environmental control of disease. We need to apply those aspects of preventive medicine which are based on genuine scientific knowledge and, at the same time, try to learn more about the basic causes, mechanisms, and treatment of our major killers by exploring them with the remarkable new tools of the basic biological sciences. The way forward must be through this two-pronged approach; to ignore either would be to reduce our chances of controlling these diseases in the long term.

REFERENCES

Ames, B. N. (1988). Endogenous oxidative DNA damage, ageing and cancer. *Free Radical Research Communications*, **7**, 121–8.

Avery, D. T., Macleod, C. M., and McCarty, M. (1944). Studies on the chemical nature of the substance inducing transformation of pneumococcal types. Induction of transformation by a deoxyribonucleic acid fraction isolated from pneumococcus type III. *Journal of Experimental Medicine*, **79**, 137–58.

Beadle, G. W. (1964). Genes and chemical reactions in *Neurospora*. Nobel Lecture, December 11th 1958. In *Nobel Lectures, Physiology and Medicine 1942–1962*, pp. 587–99. Elsevier, Amsterdam.

Bell, J. (1992). ACE (or PNMT?) in the hole. *Human Molecular Genetics*, **1**, 147–8.

Bowler, P. J. (1989). *The Mendelian revolution*. Johns Hopkins University Press, Baltimore, MD.

Brown, M. S. and Goldstein, J. L. (1988). Receptor mediated pathway for cholesterol synthesis. *Science*, **232**, 34–47.

Chen, Z., Peto, R., Collins, R., MacMahon, S., Lu., J., and Li, W. (1991). Serum cholesterol and coronary artery disease in a population with low-cholesterol concentrations. *British Medical Journal*; **303**, 276–82.

Chui, K. C., Province, M. A., and Permott, M. A. (1992). Glucokinase gene is a genetic marker for NIDDM in American Blacks. *Diabetes*, **41**, 843–9.

Doll, R. and Peto, R. (1981). *The causes of cancer*. Oxford University Press.

Flint, J., Harding, R. M., Boyce, A. J., and Clegg, J. B. (1993). The population genetics of the haemoglobinopathies. *Clinical Haematology* **6**, 215–62.

Frougel, P., Zouali, H., Vionnet, N., Velho, G., Vaxillaire, M., Sun, F., *et al.* (1993) Familial hyperglycemia due to mutations of glucokinase. *New England Journal of Medicine*, **328**, 697–703.

Garrod, A. E. (1908). *Inborn errors of metabolism: the Croonian Lecture delivered before the Royal College of Physicians of London in June, 1908*. Frowde, Hodder and Stoughton, London.

Garrod, A. E. (1923). Glimpses of the higher medicine. Linacre Lecture delivered at Cambridge on 5th May, 1923. *Lancet* **i**: 1091–6.

Garrod, A. E. (1931). *The inborn factors in disease. An essay*. Oxford University Press.

Groop, L. C., Kankuri, M., Schalin-Jäntti, R. T., Ekstrand, A., Nikula-Ijäs, P., Widén, E., *et al.* (1993). Association between polymorphism of the glycogen synthase gene and non-insulin-dependent diabetes mellitus. *New England Journal of Medicine* **328**, 10–14.

Haldane, J. B. S. (1949). Disease and evolution. Ricerca Scientifica, **19**, 3–10.

Hill, A. V. S. (1992). Malaria resistance genes: a natural selection. *Transactions of the Royal Society of Tropical Medicine and Hygiene*, **86**, 225–6.

Hobbs, H. H., Brown, M. S., and Goldstein, J. L. (1992). Molecular genetics of the LDL receptor gene in familial hypercholesterolemia. *Human Mutation*, **1**, 445–66.

Humphries, S. E., Green, F. R., Temple, A., Dawson, S., Henney, A., Kelleher, C. H., *et al.* (1992). Genetic factors determining thrombosis and fibrinolysis. *Annals of Epidemiology*, **2**, 371–85.

Johannsen, W. (1911). The genotype conception of heredity. *American Naturalist*, **45**, 129–39.

Leahy, J. L. and Boyd, A. E. (1993). Diabetes genes in non-insulin-dependent diabetes mellitus. *New England Journal of Medicine*, **328**, 56–7.

Lewin, R. (1989). *Human evolution.* Blackwell, Oxford.

Luzzi, G. A., Merry, A. H., Newbold, C. I., Marsh, K., Pasvol, G., and Weatherall, D. J. (1991). Surface antigen expression on *Plasmodium falciparum*-infected erythrocytes is modified in α- and β-thalassaemia. *Journal of Experimental Medicine*, **173**, 785–91.

McKeigue, P. M., Miller, G. J., and Marmot, M. G. (1989). Coronary heart disease in South Asians overseas: a review. *Journal of Clinical Epidemiology*, **42**, 597–609.

McKeown, T. (1988). *The origins of human disease.* Blackwell, Oxford.

Mourant, A. E., Kopec, A. C., and Domaniewska-Sobezak, K. (1978). *Blood groups and disease.* Oxford University Press.

Neel, J. V. (1962). A 'thrifty' genotype rendered detrimental by progress? *American Journal of Human Genetics*, **14**, 353–6.

O'Brien, S. J. Ghetto legacy. *Molecular Evolution*, **1**, 209–11.

Rogers, R. A., Rogers, L. A., and Martin, L. D. (1992). How the door opened: the peopling of the New World. *Human Biology*, **64**, 281–302.

Scriver, C. R., and Childs, B. (1989). *Garrod's Inborn factors in disease.* Oxford University Press.

Scriver, C. R., Beaudet, A. L., Sly, W. S., and Valle, D. (1989).

The metabolic basis of inherited disease (6th edn). McGraw-Hill, New York.

Smith, V. (1992). Lifestyle and genes—the key factors for diabetes and the metabolic syndrome. *Journal of Internal Medicine*, **232**, 99–101.

Spielman, R. S. and Nussbaum, R. L. (1992). Dual development in diabetes. *Nature and Genetics* **1**, 82–3.

Tanner, M. J. A. (1993). The major integral proteins of the human red cell. *Clinical Haematology* **6**, 333–56.

Tybjaerg-Hansen, A. and Humphries, S. E. (1992). Familial defective apolipoprotein B-100: a single mutation that causes hypercholesterolemia and premature coronary artery disease. *Atherosclerosis*, **96**, 91–107.

Watson, J. D. and Crick, F. H. C. (1953). Molecular structure of nucleic acids. *Nature, London*, **171**, 737–8.

Weatherall, D. J. (1991). *The new genetics and clinical practice*, 3rd edn. Oxford University Press.

Weatherall, D. J., Bell, J. I., Clegg, J. B., Flint, J., Higgs, D. R., Hill, A. V. S., *et al.* (1988). Genetic factors as determinants of infectious disease transmission in human communities. *Philosophical Transactions of the Royal Society of London B*, **321**, 327–48.

Weiss, K. M., Ferrell, R. E., and Harris, C. L. (1984). A New World syndrome of metabolic diseases with a genetic and evolutionary basis. *Yearbook of Physical Anthropology*, **27**, 153–78.

Zimmet, P., Dowse, G., Finch, C., Serjeantson, S., and King, H. (1990). The epidemiology and natural history of NIDDM; lessons from the South Pacific. *Diabetes and Metabolism Review*, **6**, 91–124.

8

How will it all end?

David Smith

Sir David Smith, FRS, FRSE, became President of Wolfson College, Oxford, in 1994. As a founder-member and now Honorary Fellow of Linacre College, which established and arranges these series of lectures on environmental issues, he is a doubly welcome contributor to 'Health and the environment'.

Sir David took his first degree and received his Doctorate at The Queen's College, Oxford and was appointed to a University Lectureship in the Department of Agriculture in 1960; from 1964 to 1971 he also held a Royal Society Research Fellowship at Wadham College, Oxford. After three years at Wadham as a Tutorial Fellow, Sir David moved to the University of Bristol to take up the Professorship of Botany; he subsequently combined this post with that of Director on Biological Studies. In 1980 he returned to Oxford on his appointment to the Sibthorpian Professorship of Rural Economy, which he held until 1987. In that year, Sir David was elected Principal and Vice-Chancellor of the University of Edinburgh and held office for nearly seven years. He has held numerous national honorary appointments, including the Chairmanship of two Committees of the Natural Environment Research Council. He was awarded the Linnean Medal in 1989 and has written extensively on symbiosis.

When Sir David was first invited to deliver the final lecture in the series on 'Health and the environment', it seemed that his would also be the final Linacre Lecture. Sponsorship of the Lectures, by the Racal Electronics Group, was due to end with this third series and no successor sponsor had then been found. Linacre College therefore suggested to Sir David that his lecture might be the occasion for drawing the threads together from all three series—'Monitoring the environment', 'Energy and the environment', and 'Health and the environment'—and for offering some final conclusions. Sir David agreed and framed his contribution accordingly. However, by the time that his lecture was delivered, the continuation of the Linacre Lectures for at least three further series had been assured by the generosity of British Petroleum plc. Consequently, Sir David's magisterial summing-up was in a sense premature, but he and Linacre College agreed that his lecture should nevertheless be delivered unchanged—both because an overview of the issues raised during the previous three years was in any case timely and because the message of his lecture was valuable in its own right. His audience enthusiastically endorsed this judgement.

INTRODUCTION

The answer to the question posed by the title of this chapter is reasonably clear-cut in the geological long term. The sun is about half way through its predicted life-span as a main sequence star, so that in about five billion years it will begin to run out of hydrogen fuel (which it consumes at the rate of 600 million tons of hydrogen per second). As it changes into a red giant, dramatic changes will occur: a hundred-fold increase in size, a thousand-fold increase in brightness, and the probable engulfment of this planet.

In the geological medium term, we know that the slow progressive increase in the brightness of the sun, which has been happening ever since its formation, will continue until a point is reached where a blanket of greenhouse gases will no longer be required to maintain the earth's present temperature. This point could be as close as about 100 million years from now (Lovelock 1991), although others estimate as much as one billion years (Caldeira and Kasting 1992). Unless some hitherto unsuspected mechanism of climate regulation comes into play, greenhouse blanket gases, and especially the CO_2 essential for photosynthesis and the continuation of life, will make the earth untenably hot for us.

Setting these geological end-points on one side, and bringing our focus down to time-spans that the human mind can more easily grasp, we know that so far no previous species has permanently dominated this planet and no previous human civilization has flourished permanently. Further, nearly all other animal species which have exhibited a phase of explosive population growth like that presently shown by the human species reach a point where environmental factors (such as disease, food supply, predators) cause a rapid decline in numbers.

This brings us to the present day. Several previous Linacre Lectures have betrayed a common underlying anxiety that we may be changing the planetary environment in a way that is sowing the seeds of the premature demise of our civilization. The former Prime Minister, as Mrs Margaret Thatcher, made the following memorable statement about the environment: 'No generation has a freehold on the earth . . . all we have is a life tenancy—with a full repairing lease'. The worry about our tenancy is not so much whether we are carrying out full repairs, but whether we are accelerating the rate of dilapidation of the global property to the state where it becomes, as it were, 'unfit for human habitation'.

The purpose of these lectures, as Bryan Cartledge (1992) has pointed out, is to establish a sound and more balanced perspective on environmental change. My task in this particular lecture is not so much to speculate where environmental change will lead, but rather to assess what is realistically possible in terms of altering human activities so that environmental changes can be slowed down and deleterious consequences minimized. It will emerge from my lecture that education has a vital role to play, but a role that is not being responsibly fulfilled—and especially not by universities.

We all want the span of our present civilization to be prolonged to the point where the title of this lecture, 'How will it all end?', does not carry its present threatening short-term overtones.

HOW MUCH TIME DO WE HAVE TO ALTER HUMAN ACTIVITIES AND BEHAVIOUR?

In considering the rate at which disadvantageous environmental changes are occurring, and hence the time available to arrest them before serious and irremediable consequences occur, one must bear in mind the admonition of the late Eric Ashby (1992, p. 35):

. . . for the loudest voices in the environmental clamour come from heralds of doom, naive Utopian prophets and hellfire preachers calling for ecological repentance. They appeal to emotions more than to reason, like a criminal lawyer trying to convince a jury.

In seeking a balanced perspective of the future, few can disagree with John Mason's (1992) careful, cautious, and analytical approach to the problems of the greenhouse effect and global warming in an earlier lecture in this series. He concludes that while current best estimates of global warming are not so alarming as to warrant major strategic changes now, we may only have a breathing space of about 50 years to develop adaptive strategies in energy use, food supplies, etc.

Another author of impeccable integrity and conservative approach is Gerard Piel (1992). He develops an optimistic hypothesis that the world will reach a steady state population of about ten billion, and that the production of food and energy could, *in theory*, be sufficient to support this number. However, his analysis shows that the problems of translating this theory into practice are formidable, and the final sentence of his book states (Piel 1992, p. 328):

We have not much more than a century to find our way to the steady state adjustments of our appetites, as well as our numbers, to the finite dimensions of the planet and the vulnerable cycles of its biosphere.

Thus we may have perhaps two or three generations in which to try and and achieve the necessary changes in human behaviour and activities.

Further, with regard to climate change, it must be remembered that most discussions concentrate on the consequences of just a doubling of CO_2 in the atmosphere, for this is the benchmark of the more sophisticated general circulation models. This benchmark is likely to be reached some time in the first half of the twenty-first century. However, if the concentration of greenhouse gases continues to rise beyond that point at present rates, the consequent increase in radiative forcing may result in increases in average global temperature as high as 10°C before the end of the twenty-third century. As Cline (1991 p. 223) says:

To cut off the analysis [at] CO_2 doubling is to commit the same mistake as the man who falls off the twentieth floor and concludes as he passes the sixteenth that all will be well.

SETTING PRIORITIES IN ENVIRONMENTAL CONCERNS

Recent decades have seen an unparalleled increase in concerns about the environment, and they now present a most bewildering array: save the whale, population growth, preserve the dolphin, acid rain, protect the elephant, greenhouse warming, biodiversity decline, ozone destruction, polluting the oceans, climate change, dumping nuclear waste, pesticides and wildlife, automobile fumes, recycling, poverty, sustainable development, and so on. At first sight, this gives a rather chaotic impression of humanity thrashing around and trying to solve all problems at the same time, although not having a great deal of success with any. This confusing picture has been muddied by some exaggerated forecasts of imminent doom (such as the Club of Rome's prediction in 1970 of the exhaustion of oil supplies). Furthermore, specific environmental bandwagons, many started by the media for the most worthy of objectives, have led to some issues being seen out of all proportion. Taking the example of our diet, there is intense concern about the potential carcinogenic properties of some food additives even though natural plant products in many foods have been shown by laboratory tests to be many hundreds of times more carcinogenic (Doll 1992). The total amount of browned and burnt material (e.g. through grilling, toasting, barbecuing, etc.) eaten in a typical day is at least several hundred times more carcinogenic than that inhaled from severe air pollution. Peanut butter is a much more potent source of rodent tumours in laboratory tests than some products which are banned. In an earlier chapter, Harding (p. 18) showed that obsession with the harmful effects of radiation from nuclear power plants has led to a situation where British Nuclear Fuels has to spend £1 million to achieve the same reduction of population exposure as would be obtained if £9000 were spent on replacing inefficient hospital X-ray equipment.

Inevitably, this muddled and sometimes hysteria-ridden situation evokes a backlash from the media (with articles with titles such as 'Environmentalism run riot' (*Economist*, 8 August 1992)) and, more dangerously, from a few politicians who aggressively deny any serious risks from global warming. Common sense dictates that there is a need to set reasoned priorities for environmental concerns. There is only a finite amount of resource which can be allocated to remedying these concerns, whether it is measured in terms of time and energy of individual humans or in terms of global wealth.

Environmental priorities can be divided into first-order and second-order concerns. First-order concerns are about changes to the environment which bear a credible risk of reducing the long-term survival of civilization as we know it; second-order concerns are about deteriorations of the quality of the environment in which we live, but not necessarily constituting a long-term threat to the survival of society. Concerns about global warming and climate change are included among first-order concerns, while the loss of some forms of wildlife such as the whale, the dolphin, and the elephant is a second-order concern.

An important difference between these two categories is that it is often much easier for individuals or pressure groups to achieve specific objectives with respect to second order concerns, either through promoting legislation (e.g. Wildlife Protection Acts) or through mounting successful national or international campaigns (e.g. dumping waste at sea). It is much more difficult to deal with the first-order concerns, partly because they embrace such large issues affecting key human activities, and partly because they are surrounded by degrees of uncertainty about their future impacts which seriously weaken the political resolve needed to deal with them.

With regard to the main types of first-order concern, Doll (1992) listed three major hazards to human society, and Winkelstein (1992) conveniently labelled them as the 'three Ps':

- **pollution** by greenhouse gases with consequent climate change;
- **population** growth;
- **poverty** (especially the gap between rich and poor countries).

Poverty is included as one of the three main concerns because it exacerbates the problems of pollution and population growth, and because it is probably the largest obstacle to action being taken on a global scale to rectify the other first-order concerns.

Before considering how the future environmental dangers of the 'three Ps' can be minimized, it is worth examining the past record of change on this earth, and the lessons which can be learnt from it and from present activities of the biosphere.

LESSONS TO BE LEARNT FROM PAST GLOBAL CHANGES AND PRESENT ACTIVITIES OF THE BIOSPHERE

Living organisms can cause major changes in the atmosphere. It is important to emphasize this because many people have an inner disbelief that present-day activities can seriously affect the composition of the air we breathe.

When the earth was formed, there was no oxygen in the atmosphere. It only began to accumulate after photosynthesis evolved and after the reducing 'sinks' (especially ferric iron) had become saturated by oxygen. When oxygen did begin to accumulate in significant amounts, probably about two billion years ago, it was highly toxic to most types of organisms. From the point of view of a Precambrian microbe, it was a most lethal pollutant. However, the advent of atmospheric oxygen enabled new forms of life to appear, and it is ironic to think that animals such as ourselves evolved as a result of an early episode of major atmospheric pollution.

Further, as Lovelock (1979, 1992) has pointed out, life is responsible for other fundamental characteristics of the atmosphere. His Gaia hypothesis developed from the observation that the surface temperature and composition of the earth's atmosphere was highly anomalous for its position in the solar system. Without life, the composition of the earth's atmosphere should be about 95 per cent CO_2, 2–4 per cent nitrogen, and virtually no oxygen; such a large amount of CO_2 would give a surface temperature of 300°C, and hence no liquid water. In practice, atmospheric nitrogen is slowly turning over, primarily through the microbial processes of denitrification and nitrogen fixation, and its abundance (79 per cent) is important in maintaining atmospheric pressure, without which water would boil away. The biological processes of fixation and release of CO_2 maintain this gas at the low concentration of 0.03 per cent. This low concentration is the principal reason why, compared with neighbouring planets, the earth is much cooler than would be expected from its proximity to the sun. CO_2 is a key component of the relatively thin blanket of greenhouse gases which maintains the earth's present average surface temperature of 13°C; without any blanket the temperature would be 33°C lower, but without any life the blanket would be much thicker and the earth's surface would be about 285°C hotter than at present.

It is important to be aware of the huge dimensions of the activities of the biosphere in considering its effect on the present global environment. The vital process of photosynthesis occurs over land and water, and each year it involves taking in about eight million cubic kilometres of air so that sixty billion tons of CO_2 can be fixed (Piel 1992). Terrestrial vegetation draws about 60 000 cubic kilometres of water through its tissues to help feed the needs of photosynthesis, which produces about 120–180 billion tons of new plant material each year (balanced by a comparable amount digested or decayed, consuming oxygen and releasing CO_2 in equivalently large volumes). The microbial production of gases such as nitrogen, methane, and nitrous oxide occurs at the rate of 1–2 billion tons per year.

One of the major features of past global history is that although the brightness of the sun has increased by 25–30 per cent since the formation of the earth, the earth's temperature has kept within the relatively narrow bands required to sustain living organisms. The sun was significantly cooler when life began about 3.8 billion years ago, and the oceans would have been frozen solid if the atmosphere had contained the same low amount of CO_2 as today. However, the geological evidence is clear that they were liquid, and it is inferred that CO_2 concentrations were then significantly higher. As the sun slowly warmed, the CO_2 levels progressively reduced, partly through processes of rock weathering, and partly through the activities of living organisms—not only through photosynthesis, but also through formation by myriads of microscopic organisms of shells and other calcium carbonate structures which then became deposits such as chalk and the deep ocean sediments.

Although *average* global temperatures have remained within a relatively narrow band during most of the earth's history, at any one point on the earth's surface there have been large environmental changes. Ice ages have come and gone, sea levels have risen and fallen by tens and hundreds of metres, and shifting of tectonic plates has resulted in massive continental movements. Geology is the history of change, and as Chaloner (1990) has pointed out, the evolution of man is itself the product of change because the end of the last ice age enabled our ancestors to come out of the forest and on to the prairies.

All these past changes happened very slowly, over tens and hundreds of millions of years. The key problem presently confronting the world is that the current *rate* of change due to human activity is higher than anything previously experienced. Never before in its long history has the earth seen such an explosive growth in the population of an animal of the size and resource demands of a human being. Never before have there been such rapid changes in the photosynthetic surface of the earth through urbanization, agriculture, deforestation, desertification, and surface pollution of the oceans; since 1945, 10 per cent of the vegetation-bearing surface of the earth has suffered moderate to extreme degradation (World Resources 1992). It has been estimated that human beings already appropriate about 40 per cent of the world's net primary production for their own use (Vitousek 1986). Another measure of the devastating impact of human beings on the biosphere is that the current rate of reduction of biodiversity is unparalleled over the past 65 million years. As pointed out in a joint statement by the Royal Society and the National Academy of Sciences of the USA in 1992, this loss of biodiversity is one of the fastest moving aspects of global change, it is irreversible, and it has serious consequences for human prospects in the future.

To illustrate why it is the *rate* of change which poses danger, let us consider the effects of the unprecedently rapid rise in atmospheric CO_2 due to human utilization of fossil fuels. If all the proven reserves of such fuels were to be burnt to exhaustion over the next few centuries, the CO_2 content of the atmosphere would increase about six to ten fold, probably resulting in a rise in average global temperature of 10°C. This would return us to the climate of the Mid-Cretaceous about 100 million years ago, when dinosaurs roamed the world, there were no polar ice-caps, and sea levels were very different from the present (Hoffert 1992). It is very unlikely that civilization could withstand such a rapid and traumatic change. However, many other forms of life would continue, and the earth would slowly return to its present stable state as it did after the Cretaceous.

Incidentally, this illustrates the dangers of taking an anthropocentric view of the Gaia hypothesis, and assuming that some as yet undiscovered process of global self-regulation will come into play to keep the world environment suitable for the existence of human society. As Lovelock himself has reminded us (Gribbin 1990; Lovelock 1992), Gaia will look after herself, even if that means getting rid of the human race.

THE NEED TO REDUCE RATES OF ANTHROPOGENIC ENVIRONMENTAL CHANGE

The present high rates of anthropogenic environmental change, and the associated problems of the 'three Ps', set the constraints of two or three generations as the likely maximum amount of time left to bring about the appropriate alterations in human activity and behaviour.

Of course, awareness of the threats posed by the rapid increases in pollution and population, and the association of these with poverty, is now very widespread and there is no shortage of rhetoric on how to deal with them. Unfortunately, translation of rhetoric into successful action has been very limited. Many conferences and idealistic manifestos from a variety of pressure groups and 'green' organizations have had relatively little practical effect. A shining exception was the Montreal Convention which dealt with the specific and manageable issue of the release of chlorofluorocarbons (CFCs). However, the much vaunted Rio Summit brought disappointment to many. Population and poverty were scarcely considered; a climate convention was signed by all participating nations, although its impact may be small.

As far as pollution is concerned, realistic ideas are being canvassed: carbon taxes, tradeable pollution permits, and a groundswell in favour of international negotiations to deal with the environment along the GATT pattern for international trade (Grubb *et al.* 1991; Victor 1991; Tickell 1992). However, there is little prospect of these being translated into working schemes except in a very few countries, and one is inclined to agree with Cowie (1992, p. 71) that '. . . the environmental bandwagon has had little impact on politician's work save perhaps on their rhetoric even at an international level'. This is not surprising, given the data that Cowie quotes showing that many other concerns come above the environment in the public's mind.

Other factors are also inhibitory to substantial action. Preoccupation with short-term issues such as the recession and unemployment completely swamps the essentially longer-term nature of serious environmental issues. In discussing the effect of climate change on population, (Keyfitz 1992, p. 161) states:

A part of what makes it difficult for . . . the public to attend to [the problem] is the other things that are happening . . . such matters as wars, civil disturbances, and economic fluctuations . . . mere short term effects that distract attention. They will be forgotten soon, while population growth marches inexorably on. Yet these short term disturbances do enormous damage, both directly and by exacerbating the long term problems.

Even when environmental issues are raised nationally, there is considerable confusion over the real 'costs' of various environmental remedies, which is not helped by the difficulty that lay people have in understanding the work of economists in this area, nor by an attitude prevalent amongst some environmentalists that such talk of costs is irrelevant. Further, as Cairncross (1991, p. 16) states:

Up to now, no generation has carried out its fair share of planetary repairs. Each has ignored the cost which has accrued to future generations. To demand that the present generation should undertake repairs means making people pay for something they have previously regarded as free. That is why politicians who take up green causes can suddenly find themselves in dangerous territory.

Ironically, she goes on to quote J. S. Mill on the topic of the earth as the inheritance of the human race, and the fundamental obligation of government to regulate this in a civilized society.

THE KEY ROLE OF EDUCATION

Essentially, there is little prospect that human society will change the way that it behaves to meet important environmental concerns until most people believe that those changes are necessary. Only then will the decisions required achieve political popularity instead of the unpopularity that would greet them today. Achieving this change can only be through education; it cannot be through other forms of 'social engineering'.

Two types of educational process can be loosely recognized: formal and informal. 'Informal' education nowadays occurs largely through the media, including widely reported statements by political leaders and other influential persons. Organized campaigns of 'informal education' can be remarkably effective on relatively well-defined issues at the national level: witness the success of campaigns against drinking and driving in various countries such as the UK, and the speed with which explicit discussion of sexual activity has become acceptable in the media in discussions of AIDS. About fifty years ago, any government which reduced the tax on tobacco would have earned popularity. Today, such a government would be regarded as deeply irresponsible, such has been the effectiveness of campaigns to show the linkage between smoking and cancer.

However, to deal with major global issues such as those posed by the 'three Ps' it is essential that 'informal' education is backed by the considerable power of 'formal' education, especially as practised in schools, colleges, and higher education institutions. For example, in a recent debate on BBC Radio 4 (16 February 1992) the audience voted by over two to one that the Western world must reduce its standard of living to save the planet, a view surely inculcated by 'informal' education. But it is only the power of 'formal' education that will translate that view into widespread political support for previously unpopular moves.

Good examples of the power of formal education to affect human behaviour are provided by the many religious sects in the world whose more devout members forswear activities which many others enjoy. Jews fast on the Sabbath and never mix meat and dairy products; Muslims avoid alcohol and fast daily during Ramadan; Catholics will not use contraceptive devices to avoid the burden of large families. These beliefs become deeply ingrained at an early age through a mixture of a powerful 'formal' religious education, which begins early in life, and peer group pressure from their elders.

A similarly powerful kind of 'formal' education, starting with the young, is required about first-order environmental concerns. Almost as much emphasis should be given in primary education to understanding the 'three Ps' as to learning the 'three Rs'. This proposal will strike many as naive, oversimplified, and extreme, but what practical alternative can be suggested which will lead to a sufficiently rapid and substantial alteration in human and societal behaviour?

In many countries there is little doubt that those involved in primary education could carry out the role of teaching serious environmental concerns effectively. There would then be a need for secondary and then tertiary education to link into this. The specific purpose of this chapter is to concentrate on tertiary education.

THE SPECIFIC ROLE AND RESPONSIBILITIES OF TERTIARY EDUCATION

Although only a small proportion of the human population benefits from higher education, those who do are highly important because they provide most of the political and other leaders, 'opinion formers', and others who deliver 'informal' education to the rest of the world. Indeed, it is such people who would be needed to initiate the whole educational process.

Most universities believe that they have a responsibility to transmit the cultural attitudes and values appropriate to society. Many of them now list this as one of their objectives in their mission statements or corporate plans. If this is true, and if we believe that environmental concerns are of profound importance to society, then what is tertiary education actually doing to transmit the attitudes appropriate to a proper understanding of the 'three Ps'—population, pollution, and poverty?

The answer, regrettably, is very little indeed. Many institutions refer proudly to their undergraduate and postgraduate courses in environmental science, and some refer with even greater pride to their environmental research centres. But to do this is to miss the point. Such initiatives do not touch the great cohorts of students reading subjects such as languages, literature, philosophy, mathematics, and the like. Few of our environmental science courses are sufficiently interdisciplinary to deal properly and rigorously with related issues in sociology, ethics, religion, politics, and economics. Understanding global problems requires a level of academic interdisciplinarity that very few institutions ever achieve, and certainly not at the undergraduate teaching level.

How should universities, through their formal undergraduate teaching, aim to ensure that appreciation of primary environmental concerns is widely disseminated to their student body as a whole?

Just as primary and perhaps secondary education should focus on the 'three Ps' (so inculcating the technical and scientific facts about environmental problems), then I believe tertiary education should give more fundamental consideration to the 'three Es':

- economics;
- ethics;
- ecology (in the broad sense of this term).

Let me make some comments on why each of these is important.

Economics

An appreciation of economics is fundamental to an understanding of the 'three Ps'. Conventions concerning international trade and finance will be a major component of any solution to the problem of poverty. With regard to pollution, CO_2 emission is intimately linked to energy consumption, a core requirement of the industrial prosperity essential to sustaining human society. However, despite the central importance of economics, it is a discipline poorly understood by scientists and others concerned with environmental issues. The situation is not helped by the fact that the jargon of academic economics is as incomprehensible to the lay person as is the jargon of science. Further, once the barrier of jargon is penetrated, the treatment of environmental issues by many academic economists is puzzling, since they are often assigned to the category of 'externalities' and then excluded. Also puzzling to the lay person are conventions concerning calculations of gross national product (GNP), which result in apparent anomalies such as that the *Exxon Valdez* oil spill actually increased Alaska's GNP because of the massive inflow of funds to pay for cleaning up the mess.

The depletion of natural resources such as forests and fisheries is not a conventional part of national accounting, yet the depreciation of capital resources such as the factories comprising the manufacturing base which utilize those natural resources is included. The impact of present economic activities on future generations is heavily discounted on the basis of very doubtful premises, something which strikes at the root of many environmental concerns.

There is nothing inherently wrong in a country drawing upon natural resources to finance economic growth, but it is certainly wrong to use systems of information which ignore the real economic costs of such actions (Gillis 1991). It helps to obscure the fact that bad macroeconomic policies may cause serious environmental damage. Another kind of example of the consequences of bad macroeconomic policy is the imposition of tariffs by rich countries on manufactured goods produced by poor countries, for this not only increases the poverty of the latter but also the degree of environmental damage consequently caused. Similarly, bad macroeconomic policies produce the multitude of subsidies which encourage environmentally damaging activities such as logging. Governments could discover whether their policies were truly sustainable by devising national accounts which valued both natural resources and their depreciation properly, but hardly any governments currently do so.

On the crucial question of energy, Jochem and Hohmeyer (1992, p. 234) state:

... we are all—in OECD and developing nations alike—subsidizing our present low market prices of conventional energy sources by not accounting for their true social costs. We are allowing parties who do consume less energy to subsidize those with higher levels of energy consumption. By doing this, we are wasting energy at the expense of future generations.

With regard to the medium-term effects of climate change, Nordhaus (1991) argues that it will have little effect on industry but much on agricultural production, so that developing countries will be more vulnerable than the developed world. Thus there is the danger of a situation arising in which, as Schelling (1991) points out, the countries which can afford to do something will perceive very little interest in doing so, while those which are vulnerable will have no resources to invest in their urgent needs.

Certainly, there are now some highly respected practitioners of the relatively new subject of environmental economics (Barbier 1988; Pearce and Turner 1990), but their contributions have yet to have the required impact on either mainstream economics or mainstream 'environmentalism'. The gulf between scientists and economists is well illustrated by a recent book on environmental economics (Dornbusch and Poterba 1991) in which one particular chapter (Nordhaus 1991) was praised as 'masterly' by an economist reviewer (Beckerman 1992) but dismissed as 'myopic speculation' by a scientist reviewer (Grubb 1992).

It is very much the duty of higher education to integrate economics more effectively into the array of disciplines concerned with the environment. It is sad, for example, that so very few universities can provide interdisciplinary courses on the environment for undergraduates which have an adequate content of economics to match the treatment of scientific and technical issues. Indeed, the poor representation of economics in each of these series of Linacre Lectures is sad.

Ethics

Primary environmental concerns raise fundamental ethical questions such as the nature of our obligations to future generations and to other organisms on the planet. Modern economists clearly state that it is not part of their discipline to make value judgements. However, it should not be forgotten that economics has its roots in moral philosophy (Gillis 1991), and the distinguished economist A. K. Sen has argued that modern economics has been impoverished by the distance which has grown between economics and ethics.

A central ethical issue in controversies over natural resource use and the environment is that of intergenerational equity. To what extent should current decisions affecting the environment and its exhaustible resources reflect the interests of generations to follow? Indeed, how can these interests be identified or defined? Some economists propose that environmental issues should enjoy a special low discount rate all of their own, but others (Cairncross 1991) argue that, for many environmental decisions, the whole notion of discount rates is flawed and that ultimately it is easier to think in terms of ethics than of discount rates.

Broome (1992) has analysed the problem of global warming and the issues that it raises for justice and well-being between the generations. He concludes that the changes brought about by global warming are likely to be very large and to take place over long periods of time; the associated changes in climate are hard to predict and the effects on human life even more so. He argues that these features put the problem of global warming beyond the normal experience of economics. The established methods of economics such as cost–benefit analysis cannot be applied sensibly, and one cannot rely on any of the standard techniques for setting a discount rate. Therefore governments should not think that decisions on actions to be taken in response to the prospect of global warming should be governed by straightforward techniques such as cost–benefit analysis. However, Broome also finds that if economics is discarded, a purely philosophical analysis of the concepts of justice, rights, and well-being between the generations raises particularly difficult issues. Nevertheless, there is undoubtedly an urgent need for an ethical framework to be developed to inform economic judgements. Economics by itself cannot provide answers to ethical dilemmas.

A formal understanding of ethics comes from religion and/or philosophy. Given that the majority of students do not practise a religion, then there may be particular merit in reconsidering the practice of universities a couple of centuries ago, when philosophy was an obligatory part of the curriculum. Apart from the fact that philosophy is an excellent discipline for teaching students to think and to argue, it would be a very good vehicle for introducing ethics. It should also provide a clear and more rational framework for considering issues such as limiting population growth and the preservation of biodiversity. Sadly, a formal and rigorous treatment of 'environmental ethics' scarcely features in undergraduate education.

Ecology

Too many people adopt the narrow definition that ecology deals with relationships of plants and animals to their environment. This narrow definition leads to a false dichotomy between economics and ecology. A broader and more useful definition is 'a study of plants, or of animals, or of peoples and institutions, in relation to environment' (*Chambers English Dictionary* 1988).

Such a definition clearly links ecology to economics. It renders more accessible the concept that good economics should also be good ecology, and that major man-made ecological disasters have also been economic disasters. For example, some major irrigation schemes have had devastating environmental consequences (e.g. the Aral Sea) because near-zero prices were charged for the water. In the case of tropical deforestation, popular discussions often focus on a supposed clash between economics and broader social values in tropical forest use. In practice, *economic* arguments against deforestation are available which are powerful even when a discount rate (much maligned by environmentalists) is deployed (Gillis 1991). As Prance (1992) pointed out in an earlier Linacre Lecture, Amazonian forest soils do not make good pastureland because the soil compacts too easily. Deforestation is only viable with government subsidies, and if depletion of natural resources is properly included into national accounting, then such subsidies become revealed as *economically* disastrous.

Taking the broad view of the definition of ecology also brings in the essential factor of the *costs* of environmental remedies and the fact that there is only a finite amount of resource for dealing with environmental problems. Hence choices have to be made about priorities. For example, as Cairncross (1991) points out, 'greens' need to ask whether the money that the world may yet spend to check global warming might yield larger environmental benefits if vested elsewhere—on population control or preservation of endangered species. To think of the environment in economic terms is not only useful to environmentalists, but also helpful to businessmen and politicians.

Above all, integrating the broad view of ecology with economics helps to improve understanding of the true limits to growth. According to Cairncross, these are not the earth's stock of natural resources such as coal, oil, and iron, which are bought and sold at prices that will rise to reflect increasing scarcity. Rather, the true limits to growth are the capacity of the environment to deal with waste in all its forms and the 'critical' resources, such as the ozone layer, the carbon cycle, and the Amazon forests, which play no direct role in world commerce yet which serve the most basic economic function of all, which is to enable human beings to survive.

There is an urgent need to understand and teach the fundamental nature of global ecology (including the involvement of people and institutions) as a complex set of interrelationships. Lovelock's Gaia hypothesis, although criticized by some for likening the world to a living organism, nevertheless illustrates the type of interdisciplinary approach which is necessary. When integrating human society into this approach, proper appreciation of its economic activities should recognize, for example, the importance of multinational corporations, for they are responsible for about 30 per cent of global GNP yet are not answerable to any democratic control beyond their shareholders (Piel 1992). Multinational Corporations *are* an important component of global ecology!

BRINGING ABOUT THE NECESSARY CHANGE IN HIGHER EDUCATION

Bringing about radical change in higher education is never easy, but it is possible. Recent experience at the University of Edinburgh illustrates both the problems and the potential.

The Principal of the University began by writing an article in the University's internal newsletter in December 1990. After arguing the urgency and complexity of threats to the global environment, he wrote:

All activities of the University should be examined to explore whether an integrated 'environmental initiative' could be developed, partly analogous to the current 'enterprise initiative' but also extending into spheres other than teaching. An integrated environmental initiative would include not only teaching and research, but also the ways in which these link with environmental aspects of how the institution itself operates—'institutional behaviour'.

The proposal received wide support, and a framework was established for implementing the initiative. It was important for the framework to be embedded into the central committee structure of the University, and not marginalized as a fringe activity. Three groups were established: an Environmental Teaching Group (as a subcommittee of the University's Educational Policy Committee), an Environmental Research Group (as a subcommittee of the University's Research Committee), and an Energy and Environment Group, which developed from a pre-existing Energy Conservation Group (which had already successfully achieved substantial economies on the University's energy budget). The activities of the three groups were co-ordinated by a body consisting of the three conveners chaired by the Senior Vice-Principal (who had delegated responsibility from the Principal for the whole initiative). Additionally, valuable academic support for the initiative came from the University's Centre for Human Ecology (which originated from the late C. H. Waddington's 'School of the Man-Made Future', formed in the 1960s).

The most innovative aspect of the initiative concerned teaching, for the Educational Policy Committee had agreed that:

All undergraduates, at some time in their course, should be exposed to teaching about the wider and more fundamental issues of society's relationship to the environment, including complex social, economic and ethical questions, as well as some understanding of basic technical issues.

The first stage in implementing this policy was to make a detailed survey throughout the University, department by department, of courses which included environmental concerns. The Centre for Human Ecology was commissioned to carry out the survey, and it was assisted by the fact that each of the eight faculties appointed a Faculty Environmental Co-ordinator to liaise with the centre. Sixty-nine departments or other teaching units completed a questionnaire covering the following topics: the extent to which existing teaching integrated environmental awareness; the potential for extending and developing this; the present situation and future potential for moving beyond traditional didactic approaches; the human and material resource consequences of greater environmental integration in teaching.

The survey (Centre for Human Ecology 1991) found wide (but scattered) interest. Over two hundred courses were listed, of which the environmental content was self-assessed as 'high' in sixty, 'medium' in fifty, and 'low' in ninety. A number of negative influences emerged: severe resource constraints would prove a major stumbling block; the rate of radical change would be slow; many subjects were considered of no relevance to ecology; the curriculum was already full and further expansion was undesirable. Therefore it was decided that an evolutionary or 'contextualized' approach to environmental education would be most appropriate. This would first involve 'consciousness-raising' amongst those who had not previously appreciated the breadth of implications of environmental thought or practice, nor therefore the relevance of environmental issues to their own disciplines. A broadening of vision from one discipline to others with ecological significance would help to break down some long-standing barriers, such as the rigid two cultures divide between arts and science (the latter still being viewed as the main repository for environmental knowledge). Few scientists, for example, are aware of the depth to which relevant environmental issues are taught in departments such as law, politics, economics, architecture, economic and social history, geography, nursing studies, politics, social anthropology, sociology, archaeology, philosophy, etc. The next stage in the work of the Teaching Group will be a practical consideration of how best to structure flexible multidisciplinary degree curricula with a high environmental content.

The work of the Research Group has followed along the parallel line of first surveying current activities in the institution (including listing more than 130 staff distributed across almost all faculties with research interest in environmental issues). It will then actively promote further developments, particularly of an interdisciplinary nature. The Energy and Environment Group, starting from a record of substantial success in reducing the University's energy bill (currently just over £3 million per annum) has now expanded into a wider range of matters such as recycling and waste management schemes and purchasing policies. It operates through a forum which includes students and trade unions.

Three conclusions can be drawn from the experience of the University of Edinburgh.

(1) It is vital that there should be total commitment from those who lead the institution.
(2) It is important that an initiative should be seen to be integrated and co-ordinated across all aspects of an institution's activities, and especially across the breadth of its undergraduate teaching.
(3) Even so, the innate conservatism of universities means that change will be slow, so that the evolutionary approach will be more successful than the revolutionary.

The University has a very long way to go before reaching the idealized kind of curriculum adumbrated earlier in this chapter, but at least it has begun.

CONCLUSIONS

Education—primary, secondary, and tertiary—will have a key role in helping to bring about the necessary change in attitude for there to be popular support for measures to address the threats of the 'three Ps'. Bringing about this change on a global scale over the next generation or so is a formidable challenge, and it will stand no chance without the support of major political figures. In this respect, it is profoundly encouraging that the Vice-President of the USA has written a remarkable book (Gore 1992) which not only reveals an enviable grasp of the scientific and technical aspects of the primary environmental concerns confronting the world, but also outlines some politically realistic ways of dealing with them. While it is quite naive to imagine that much of what he wrote will be put into practice during the first period of the Clinton administration, at least there is hope.

The universities and their academic staff have their own role to play. If they are willing to accept that they have not really faced up to their responsibilities hitherto, then that will be a first step—but the first step along a lengthy path that must be traversed within a couple of generations.

The simple answer to the question posed by the title of this chapter, 'How will it all end?' is 'It depends on us'.

REFERENCES

Ashby, E. (1992). Sanity for the 21st century. Review of *Only one world* by Gerard Piel. *New Scientist*, no. 1837, 5 September.

Barbier, E. B. (1988). *New approaches in environmental economics*. International Institute for Environment and Development, London.

Beckerman, W. (1992). The environment as a commodity. Review of *Global warming: economic policy responses*, ed. by R. Dornbusch and J. H. Poterba, *Nature, London*, **357**, 371–2.

Broome, J. (1992). *Counting the cost of global warming*. Whitehorse Press, Cambridge.

Cairncross, F. (1991). *Costing the earth*. Economist Books, London.

Caldeira, K. and Kasting, J. F. (1992). The life span of the biosphere revisited. *Nature, London*, **360**, 721–3.

Cartledge, B. (1992). Introduction. In *Monitoring the environment* (ed. B. Cartledge), pp. 1–4. Oxford University Press.

Centre for Human Ecology, University of Edinburgh. (1991). *Environmental education for adaptation*. Internal Report.

Chaloner, W. (1990). Global change: the past as a key to the future. *Science and Public Affairs*, **5**, 3–10.

Cline, W. R. (1991). Comments. In *Global warming: economic policy responses* (ed. R. Dornbusch and J. M. Poterba), pp. 222–8., MIT Press, Cambridge, MA.

Cowie, J. (1992). Of environmental bandwagons. *Biologist*, **39**, 70–1.

Doll, R. (1992). Health and the environment in the 1990s. *American Journal of Public Health*, **82** 933–41.

Dornbusch, R. and Poterba, J. M. (ed.). (1991). *Global warming: economic policy responses*. MIT Press, Cambridge, MA.

Gillis, M. (1991). Ecology, economics, ethics: mending the broken circle for tropical forests. In *Ecology, economics, ethics: the broken circle* (ed. F. H. Bormann and S. R. Kellert), pp. 155–79. Yale University Press, New Haven, CT. Gore, A. (1992).

Gribbin, J. (1990). *Hothouse earth: the greenhouse effect and Gaia*. Bantam Press, London.

Grubb, M. (1992). Climate change. *Nature, London*, **358**, 448.

Grubb, M., Victor, D. G., and Hope, C. W. (1991). Pragmaticss in the greenhouse. *Nature, London*, **354**, 348–53.

Hoffert, M. I. (1992). Climate sensitivity, climate feedbacks and policy implications. In *Confronting climate change* (ed. I. M. Mintzer), pp. 33–54. Cambridge University Press.

Jochem, E. and Hohmeyer, O. (1992). The economics of near-term reductions in greenhouse gases. In *Confronting climate change* (ed. I. M. Mintzer), pp. 217–36. Cambridge University Press.

Keyfitz, N. (1992). The effect of changing climate on population. In *Confronting climate change* (ed. I. M. Mintzer), pp. 153–61. Cambridge University Press.

Lovelock, J. E. (1979). *Gaia: a new look at life on earth*. Oxford University Press.

Lovelock, J. E. (1988). *The ages of Gaia: a biography of our living earth*. Oxford University Press.

Lovelock, J. E. (1991). *Gaia: the practical science of planetary management*. Gaia Books, London.

Lovelock, J. E. (1992). The earth is not fragile. In *Monitoring the Environment* (ed. B. Cartledge), pp. 105–22. Oxford University Press.

Lovelock, J. E. and Whitfield, M. (1982). *Nature, London*, **296**, 561–3.

Mason, J. (1992). The greenhouse effect and global warming. In *Monitoring the environment* (ed. B. Cartledge), pp. 55–92. Oxford University Press.

Nordhaus, W. D. (1991). Economic approaches to greenhouse warming. In *Global warming: economic policy responses* (ed. R. Dornbusch and J. M. Poterba), pp. 33–66. MIT Press, Carnbridge, MA.

Pearce, D. W. and Turner, K. (1990). *Economics of natural resources and the environment*. Harvester Wheatsheaf, Hemel Hempstead.

Piel, G. (1992). *Only one world: our own to make and keep*. W. H. Freeman, New York.

Prance, G. T. (1992). The dilemma of the Amazon rainforests: biological reserve or exploitable resource? In *Monitoring the Environment* (ed. B. Cartledge), pp. 157–92. Oxford University Press.

Schelling, T. C. (1991). Economic responses to global warming: prospects for cooperative approaches. In *Global warming: economic policy responses* (ed. R. Dornbusch and J. M. Poterba), pp. 197–221. MIT Press, Cambridge, MA.

Tickell, C. (1992). Implications of global climatic change. In *Monitoring the Environment* (ed. B. Cartledge), pp. 93–104. Oxford University Press.

Victor, D. G. (1991). How to slow global warming. *Nature, London*, **349**, 451–6.

Vitousek, P. (1986). Human appropriation of the products of photosynthesis. *Bioscience*, June.

Winkelstein, W. (1992). Determinants of worldwide health. *American Journal of Public Health*, **82**, 931–2. World Resources (1992).

Index